Gluten-Free Cookbook:

Delicious and Nourishing Recipes for a Healthy Lifestyle

Verity Everhart

© **Copyright 2024 - All rights reserved.**

The contents of this book may not be reproduced, duplicated, or transmitted without the direct written permission of the author or publisher.

Under no circumstances will the publisher or author be held liable for any damages, recovery, or financial loss due to the information contained in this book. Neither directly nor indirectly.

Legal Notice:

This book is protected by copyright. This book is for personal use only. You may not modify, distribute, sell, use, quote, or paraphrase any part or content of this book without the permission of the author or publisher.

Disclaimer Notice:

Please note that the information contained in this document is for educational and entertainment purposes only. Every effort has been made to present accurate, current, reliable, and complete information. No warranties of any kind are stated or implied. The reader acknowledges that the author is not offering legal, financial, medical, or professional advice. The contents of this book have been taken from various sources. Please consult a licensed professional before attempting any of the techniques described in this book.

By reading this document, the reader agrees that under no circumstances will the author be liable for any direct or indirect loss arising from the use of the information contained in this document, including but not limited to - errors, omissions, or inaccuracies.

Table of Contents

Chapter 1 Understanding Gluten and Its Impact 7

Chapter 2 Navigating the Gluten-Free Pantry 20

Chapter 3 Setting the Foundation 34

Chapter 4 Morning Bliss: Gluten-Free Breakfast Delights 41

    Quinoa Breakfast Bowl 41

    Gluten-Free Banana Pancakes 42

    Greek Yogurt Parfait 42

    Sweet Potato Hash with Eggs 43

    Chia Seed Pudding 43

    Gluten-Free Zucchini Muffins 44

    Spinach and Feta Omelette 45

    Gluten-Free Breakfast Burrito 45

    Gluten-Free Blueberry Muffins 46

    Gluten-Free Avocado Toast 47

Chapter 5 Lunchtime Sensations: Flavorful Gluten-Free Creations 48

    Quinoa Salad with Lemon Herb Dressing 48

    Grilled Chicken and Vegetable Skewers 48

    Gluten-Free Caprese Pasta Salad 49

    Stuffed Bell Peppers with Quinoa and Black Beans 50

    Gluten-Free Chicken and Vegetable Stir-Fry 50

    Gluten-Free Spinach and Feta Stuffed Chicken Breast 51

    Gluten-Free Shrimp and Quinoa Bowl 52

    Gluten-Free Turkey and Vegetable Lettuce Wraps 53

    Gluten-Free Eggplant Parmesan 53

Gluten-Free Teriyaki Salmon Bowl 54

Chapter 6 Dinner Elegance: Gourmet Gluten-Free Fare 56

Lemon Garlic Herb Roast Chicken 56

Gluten-Free Shrimp Scampi with Zoodles 56

Gluten-Free Mushroom Risotto 57

Gluten-Free Beef Tenderloin with Red Wine Reduction 58

Gluten-Free Lobster Tail with Garlic Butter 59

Gluten-Free Butternut Squash and Sage Risotto 59

Gluten-Free Salmon with Dill Sauce 60

Gluten-Free Beef and Vegetable Stir-Fry 61

Gluten-Free Chicken Marsala 62

Gluten-Free Eggplant and Goat Cheese Stacks 63

Chapter 7 Baking Without Limits: Irresistible Gluten-Free Treats 64

Gluten-Free Chocolate Chip Cookies 64

Gluten-Free Blueberry Muffins 65

Gluten-Free Banana Bread 66

Gluten-Free Lemon Bars 66

Gluten-Free Chocolate Cake 67

Gluten-Free Apple Crisp 68

Gluten-Free Pumpkin Bread 69

Gluten-Free Raspberry Almond Bars 70

Gluten-Free Chocolate Avocado Mousse 71

Gluten-Free Cookies 72

Chapter 8 International Flavors, Gluten-Free Style 73

Thai Basil Chicken (Pad Krapow Gai) 73

Mango and Avocado Salsa with Shrimp Tacos 74

Indian Butter Chicken (Murgh Makhani) 74

Greek Quinoa Salad with Lemon Herb Dressing 75

Japanese-inspired Miso Glazed Salmon 76

Mexican Quinoa Stuffed Peppers 77

Italian-inspired Caprese Chicken 78

Moroccan-inspired Quinoa Tagine 78

Brazilian-inspired Chicken Coxinha 80

Spanish-inspired Paella with Chorizo and Seafood 81

Chapter 9 Hearty and Wholesome: Gluten-Free Comfort Foods 83

Gluten-Free Chicken and Rice Casserole 83

Gluten-Free Beef Stew 84

Gluten-Free Spinach and Feta Stuffed Chicken Breasts 84

Gluten-Free Turkey and Vegetable Meatloaf 85

Gluten-Free Chicken and Broccoli Alfredo Bake 86

Gluten-Free Sweet Potato and Black Bean Chili 87

Gluten-Free Shepherd's Pie 88

Gluten-Free Quinoa and Vegetable Stir-Fry 89

Gluten-Free Eggplant Parmesan 89

Gluten-Free Chicken Pot Pie 91

Chapter 10 Sweet Endings: Delectable Gluten-Free Desserts 93

Gluten-Free Chocolate Chip Cookies 93

Gluten-Free Flourless Chocolate Cake 94

Gluten-Free Lemon Bars 94

Gluten-Free Almond Flour Brownies 95

Gluten-Free Raspberry Cheesecake Bars 96

Gluten-Free Apple Crisp 97

Gluten-Free Peanut Butter Blossoms 98

Gluten-Free Banana Bread 99

Gluten-Free Blueberry Muffins... 100

Gluten-Free Chocolate Avocado Mousse 101

Conclusion **102**

Chapter 1
Understanding Gluten and Its Impact

- The Basics of Gluten: What is Gluten?

Gluten, a blend of proteins found in wheat and related grains, is an essential component of cooking that gives various dishes their distinct flavors and textures as well as their structural integrity. Essentially, gluten is a complex protein mixture that is intricately woven into the texture of wheat, barley, rye, and oats. The primary proteins in this mixture are gliadin and glutenin (often contaminated during processing).

When flour, the primary source of gluten, comes into touch with moisture, a changing process begins. This contact results in the formation of a viscoelastic network, an essential ingredient in baking inventiveness. This network helps bread rise and acquire that much-desired fluffy texture by allowing dough to stretch and retain the gasses released by leavening agents.

The molecular structure formed by the combination of glutenin and gliadin is greatly changed by mechanical forces (such kneading or mixing). Gluten is necessary for the creation of many delicious dishes, such as artisanal bread and delicate pastries, because it makes the dough elastic and cohesive.

But because gluten is present in many foods, it might be problematic for people who have celiac disease or gluten sensitivity. People who suffer from these illnesses need to understand the nuances of gluten. Gliadin, a protein found in gluten, can trigger an immune response in celiac disease sufferers that destroys and inflames the small intestine.

In addition to its common usage in baking, gluten has been used into a broad variety of processed foods, providing structure, texture, and stabilizing properties. As the public becomes more aware of the health risks associated with gluten, so does the need for gluten-free alternatives and a fuller understanding of the intricate characteristics of this composite protein.

In short, gluten is proof that science and creativity can work together in the kitchen, not simply a component. Its intricacy not only elucidates the characteristics of beloved recipes but also sparks a deeper conversation on dietary choices, health issues, and the evolving nature of modern cuisine.

- Sources of Gluten in Common Foods

For those with celiac disease or gluten sensitivity, navigating the confusing world of gluten-containing foods is crucial. Because of its special qualities, gluten—a compound of proteins present in some grains—is a versatile component that is frequently employed in the culinary arts. This is a detailed investigation of typical foods that contain gluten:

1. Wheat and Its Derivatives:
   - **Bread and Baked Goods:** Wheat flour, a major source of gluten, is essential to making traditional bread, rolls, bagels, and pastries. The distinctive structure of these items is derived from the network of gluten that forms during baking.
   - **Pasta:** The majority of pasta products are prepared using wheat semolina, which adds to the gluten content unless they are specifically labeled as gluten-free.
2. Barley and Barley Products:
   - **Malt:** Made from germinated barley grains, barley malt is frequently added to a variety of culinary goods as a sweetener or flavor enhancer. It is inappropriate for people who are avoiding gluten because to its high gluten level.
   - **Beer:** Unless specifically marked as gluten-free, traditional beer is made with barley, which introduces gluten into the drink during the fermentation process.
3. Rye and Rye-Based Foods:
   - **Rye Bread:** With its distinct flavor and texture, rye bread is a beloved choice in many cuisines. However, its use of rye flour makes it a significant source of gluten.
   - **Rye Crackers:** Commonly found in the snack aisle, crackers made with rye flour contribute to gluten intake.
4. Oats (Potential Contaminant):
   - **Cross-Contamination Concerns:** Although oats are naturally gluten-free, cross-contamination can occur during manufacturing. It's best to purchase items branded as certified gluten-free to assure gluten-free oats.
5. Processed and Packaged Foods:
   - **Sauces and Gravies:** A common thickening additive in commercially made sauces and gravies is wheat flour. This includes traditional dishes like savory sauces for ready-to-eat meals or gravy to go with roasts.
   - **Processed Meats:** Certain processed meats, such as sausages and hot dogs, may incorporate breadcrumbs or fillers containing gluten.
6. Soups and Bouillons:
   - **Thickeners:** Canned and pre-packaged soups often use wheat-based thickeners for texture and consistency, making them potential sources of gluten.
7. Snack Foods:
   - **Pretzels and Crackers:** Popular snack items like pretzels and certain crackers are typically made with wheat flour, contributing to their crunch and texture.
   - **Granola Bars:** Many granola bars contain oats and other grains, potentially introducing gluten into these convenient, on-the-go snacks.
8. Dressings and Marinades:

- **Stabilizers and Thickeners:** Salad dressings, marinades, and condiments may contain gluten as stabilizers or thickening agents, enhancing their texture and shelf stability.
9. Desserts and Confections:
    - **Baked Goods:** Cakes, cookies, and pastries made with conventional flour contain gluten, contributing to their structure and texture.

Ice Cream Cones: Cones made from wheat flour, commonly available in ice cream shops, have a gluten content that people with special dietary needs should be aware of.

Understanding the vast array of items that have gluten requires closely reading ingredient labels and selecting gluten-free options where necessary. Knowing this helps consumers make choices that fit their nutritional needs and tastes whether they're dining out or cooking at home.

- Gluten's Role in Baking and Cooking

Gluten has an essential and fascinating role in the culinary arts, especially in baking and cooking. Certain grains contain a complex protein called gluten, which plays a crucial role in creating the various foods' textures, structures, and overall palatability. Let's now examine the intricate dance that gluten does in the kitchen:

1. Structure and Elasticity in Baking:
    - **Formation of Dough:** Gluten is formed when flour—usually wheat flour—comes into contact with fluids. Dough cannot be created without this procedure, which gives it the structure and elasticity it needs.
    - **Gas Retention:** Gluten captures gasses released during fermentation to function as a natural leavening agent. The dough rises as a result of the trapped gas, giving well-baked bread its typical airy and light quality.
2. Texture and Cohesion in Baked Goods:
    - **Chewiness in Bread:** The distinct chewiness of bread is attributed to the particular combination of gliadin and glutenin proteins in gluten. Particularly valued are bread types that are artisanal and rustic and have this texture.
    - **Flakiness in Pastries:** Gluten adds to the flakiness and delicate layers of pastries. The ideal ratio of structure to softness is largely dependent on the controlled synthesis of gluten.
3. Binding and Stability in Cooking:
    - **Binding Agents:** Gluten acts as a natural binder in cooking, keeping ingredients together. This is especially true for foods like meatballs or veggie burgers, where the gluten gives the ingredients the cohesiveness they need to form a single, cohesive structure.

- **Thickening Sauces and Gravies:** Gravies and sauces frequently use gluten as a thickening agent. It gives these food accompaniments a rich, velvety feel as it swells and absorbs liquid.
4. Enhancing Flavors and Textures:
    - **Flavor Development:** When gluten is present, the Maillard reaction—a chemical interaction between amino acids and reducing sugars—occurs more frequently. The complex flavors and rich, golden-brown color of baked foods, such as bread crusts, are a result of this reaction.
    - **Textural Variety:** Whether gluten is present or not, a variety of textures can be used in cooking. Gluten provides a wide range of sensory pleasures, from the chewiness of handcrafted bread to the delicate crumb of a cake baked to perfection.
5. Versatility in Culinary Applications:

Diverse Applications: Gluten can be used in many more culinary applications than baking. It can be used to make many different kinds of cuisine; two examples are pizza crust and pasta dough.

Understanding the role that gluten plays in baking and cooking makes the creation of food—both the art and science—more enjoyable. Although gluten contributes to the beloved flavors and textures of many meals, it's crucial to understand that in order to foster inclusivity and a diverse range of culinary experiences, gluten-free solutions are required for those with dietary restrictions or sensitivities.

- Gluten Sensitivity vs. Celiac Disease: Recognizing the Signs of Gluten Sensitivity

For those who are reacting negatively to gluten, it is critical to understand the differences between gluten sensitivity and celiac disease. Despite the fact that this protein is very sensitive in both circumstances, the mechanisms and health effects are distinct. Focusing on recognizing the signs of gluten sensitivity in particular yields useful information:

1. Gastrointestinal Symptoms:
    - **Abdominal Discomfort:** Gluten sensitivity typically presents as abdominal pain, bloating, and discomfort after consuming gluten-containing meals. Consuming goods made of wheat could make this discomfort worse.
    - **Diarrhea or Constipation:** Changes in bowel habits, which can range from constipation to diarrhea, are frequently seen signs of gluten sensitivity. Normal bowel function may be disturbed as a result of the effect on the digestive system.
2. Non-Gastrointestinal Symptoms:
    - **Fatigue and Lethargy:** Gluten-sensitive people frequently complain of ongoing exhaustion, even after getting enough sleep. The everyday activities and general quality of life may be impacted by this tiredness.

- **Headaches:** Headaches and migraines are common symptoms, and for some people, following a gluten-free diet significantly lessens or eliminates these symptoms entirely.
- **Joint Pain:** Joint discomfort may be exacerbated by gluten sensitivity even in the absence of a clear underlying cause. Daily activities and mobility may be impacted by this ache.

3. Dermatological Manifestations:
    - **Skin Issues:** Eczema, dermatitis herpetiformis (a particular skin manifestation of gluten sensitivity), and generalized skin inflammation are examples of dermatological signs that may indicate gluten sensitivity. If gluten is removed from the diet, skin issues may improve.
4. Neurological Symptoms:
    - **Brain Fog:** Cognitive symptoms are frequent in people with gluten sensitivity, and might include trouble focusing, memory problems, and a feeling of mental "fogginess." Cognitive performance may improve with a gluten-free diet.
    - **Mood Disorders:** Anxiety and depression have been linked to gluten sensitivity. Addressing gluten consumption may lead to improvements in mood and overall mental well-being.
5. Respiratory Symptoms:
    - **Nasal Congestion:** Gluten sensitivity may contribute to nasal congestion or sinus issues in some individuals. These symptoms can be exacerbated by the consumption of gluten-containing foods.
    - **Asthma-Like Symptoms:** Respiratory symptoms resembling asthma, such as wheezing or shortness of breath, may occur in response to gluten consumption.
6. Reproductive Issues:
    - **Menstrual Irregularities:** Gluten sensitivity in women might lead to erratic menstruation cycles or worsened premenstrual symptoms. Reproductive health may return to normal if gluten consumption is addressed.
7. Exclusion of Celiac Disease:

Negative Celiac Testing: Contrary to celiac disease, people with gluten sensitivity usually show negative findings on tests meant to diagnose the condition, such as blood testing and small intestinal biopsies.

It is imperative to acknowledge that the expressions of gluten sensitivity can differ significantly between people, and the lack of conclusive diagnostic procedures for this ailment means that identifying symptoms is a crucial first step towards its diagnosis. Individuals who continue to have symptoms associated with gluten sensitivity ought to consult medical authorities. Additionally, working with a trained dietitian can help create a gluten-free diet that is nutritionally sound, balanced, and customized to target certain symptoms and enhance general wellbeing.

- Understanding Celiac Disease: A Closer Look

The chronic autoimmune ailment known as celiac disease is brought on by consuming gluten, a protein present in wheat, barley, rye, and their byproducts. This illness affects the small intestine and may have a major impact on an individual's overall health. Examining celiac disease in further detail exposes its complex nature:

1. Autoimmune Response to Gluten:
   - **Immune System Activation:** Celiac disease is characterized by an inappropriate immunological reaction to gluten. When someone with celiac disease eats gluten, their immune system unintentionally targets the small intestine's lining, causing inflammation and damage.
2. Genetic Predisposition:
   - **HLA-DQ Genes:** Celiac disease is significantly influenced by genetic factors. The presence of specific genes, particularly HLA-DQtwo or HLA-DQ8, increases the probability of acquiring the illness. But not everyone who carries these genes goes on to get celiac disease.
3. Small Intestinal Damage:
   - **Villous Atrophy:** Long-term gluten exposure causes a disorder called villous atrophy, in which the small intestine's lining of tiny projections called villi flatten and resemble fingers. This can result in a variety of dietary deficits by impeding the absorption of nutrients.
4. Gastrointestinal and Non-Gastrointestinal Symptoms:
   - **Classic Symptoms:** Weight loss, diarrhea, bloating, and stomach pain are typical gastrointestinal symptoms. On the other hand, non-gastrointestinal symptoms including weariness, joint discomfort, and skin rashes can also be indicative of celiac disease.
   - **Asymptomatic Cases:** Diagnosis can be difficult since some people with celiac disease may not show any symptoms at all. These cases of celiac disease are known as "asymptomatic" or "silent."
5. Diagnosis and Testing:
   - **Blood Tests:** To screen for celiac disease, blood tests assessing certain antibodies (anti-endomysial and anti-tissue transglutaminase antibodies) are frequently performed. Increased antibody levels can be a sign that additional testing is required.
   - **Endoscopy and Biopsy:** An endoscopy with biopsy is frequently required for a conclusive diagnosis. Through this process, medical personnel can take tissue samples for microscopic analysis and physically evaluate the small intestine.
6. Treatment:

- **Strict Gluten-Free Diet:** A stringent gluten-free diet must be followed for the rest of one's life as the only therapy option for celiac disease. This entails staying away from all gluten-containing foods, such as wheat, barley, rye, and their derivatives.
- **Nutritional Support:** Depending on the extent of malabsorption, individuals with celiac disease may require nutritional supplements to address deficiencies in vitamins and minerals.

7. Complications and Long-Term Effects:
   - **Osteoporosis:** Malabsorption of calcium and vitamin D can lead to bone density loss, increasing the risk of osteoporosis.
   - **Infertility and Reproductive Issues:** Celiac disease can impact reproductive health, leading to fertility issues and complications during pregnancy.
   - **Increased Risk of Other Autoimmune Disorders:** Individuals with celiac disease have a higher likelihood of developing other autoimmune conditions.
8. Lifestyle Considerations:
   - **Social and Emotional Impact:** Managing celiac disease extends beyond dietary considerations, impacting social and emotional well-being. Negotiating social situations, dining out, and maintaining a gluten-free lifestyle can present unique challenges.

Comprehensive knowledge of the autoimmune nature of celiac disease, the influence of genetics, the variety of symptomatology, the diagnostic procedures, and the necessity of a lifelong commitment to a gluten-free lifestyle as the cornerstone of management are all necessary to comprehend the condition. With the right diagnosis, assistance, and information, people with celiac disease may manage the intricacies of their illness and enjoy happy, healthy lives.

- Importance of Proper Diagnosis and Medical Guidance

Accurate diagnosis and medical guidance are essential to the understanding and treatment of gluten-related diseases such celiac disease and gluten sensitivity. Handling these situations without the guidance of a professional might impede the development of strategies for optimal health and result in possible difficulties. Here is a look at why it's so important to get a thorough diagnosis and medical advice:

1. Precision in Treatment:
   - **Distinguishing Between Conditions:** It's important to distinguish between celiac disease and gluten sensitivity because their symptoms often overlap. Accurate diagnosis guarantees that patients receive the right care for their particular disease.
2. Avoiding Self-Diagnosis Pitfalls:
   - **Varied Presentations:** Gluten-related illnesses can present in a variety of ways, and conventional wisdom may not necessarily apply to the symptoms. Relying on

oneself for diagnosis runs the risk of misinterpreting symptoms and delaying getting the right care.
3. Identification of Underlying Conditions:
    - **Associated Health Issues:** Celiac disease is typically connected with other autoimmune illnesses, such as type one diabetes and autoimmune thyroid problems. A thorough diagnosis enables medical practitioners to recognize and manage possible coexisting health problems.
4. Preventing Nutritional Deficiencies:
    - **Malabsorption Challenges:** Untreated celiac disease can result in impaired absorption of vital nutrients. Timely intervention can be prevented by proper diagnosis, so averting dietary deficits that could have long-term repercussions.
5. Establishing a Baseline for Monitoring:
    - **Tracking Progress:** Medical guidelines offer a structure for determining a person's initial state of health and tracking their advancement over time. Healthcare providers can monitor treatment effectiveness and make necessary strategy adjustments with the support of routine examinations and assessments.
6. Accurate Management Strategies:
    - **Tailored Treatment Plans:** While managing celiac disease requires a rigorous gluten-free diet, dietary modifications may be necessary for those with gluten sensitivity. A precise diagnosis makes it possible to create individualized treatment programs that meet each patient's unique needs.
7. Emotional and Psychological Support:
    - **Navigating Lifestyle Changes:** When a gluten-related ailment is diagnosed, major lifestyle modifications are frequently required. In order to help people adjust to these changes, medical experts can provide emotional support and put them in touch with services, support groups, or mental health specialists.
8. Screening for Family Members:
    - **Genetic Considerations:** There is a genetic component to celiac disease, and family members may be more susceptible. When a diagnosis is made correctly, family members are screened for, enabling early identification and, if needed, intervention.
9. Avoiding Potential Complications:
    - **Preventing Long-Term Damage:** If left untreated, celiac disease can result in osteoporosis, infertility, and a higher chance of developing several types of cancer. Adherence to a gluten-free diet and prompt diagnosis help reduce these risks..
10. Ensuring Compliance with Dietary Restrictions:

Comprehensive Education: Health care providers are essential in teaching people about the subtleties of adopting a gluten-free lifestyle. They can offer tools, nutritional advice, and continuing assistance to improve adherence to essential dietary limitations.

In summary, getting a correct diagnosis and medical advice is essential for managing gluten-related disorders and is also fundamental to maintaining general health. Informed decision-making, encouraging a balanced and healthy lifestyle, and navigating the intricacies of chronic disorders all depend on the collaboration between individuals and healthcare professionals.

- The Health Benefits of Going Gluten-Free: Improved Digestive Health

Changing to a gluten-free diet has several health advantages, especially when it comes to digestive health. Although this is a necessary dietary option for those with gluten-related problems, people without a diagnosis may benefit from it as well. An examination of the ways in which avoiding gluten can enhance gut health is provided below:

1. Reduced Gastrointestinal Distress:
   - **Alleviation of Abdominal Discomfort:** Removing gluten from the diet usually relieves discomfort, bloating, and abdominal pain—symptoms that are commonly linked to gluten consumption—for people who have celiac disease or gluten sensitivity.
2. Normalization of Bowel Habits:
   - **Stabilization of Bowel Movements:** Going gluten-free can contribute to the stabilization of bowel habits, addressing issues such as diarrhea or constipation that may be triggered by gluten consumption.
3. Resolution of Gluten-Induced Inflammation:
   - **Reduction in Intestinal Inflammation:** When gluten is consumed, those who are gluten sensitive get mild intestinal inflammation. A gluten-free diet reduces inflammation and promotes the healing and restoration of normal function of the intestinal lining.
4. Management of Irritable Bowel Syndrome (IBS) Symptoms:
   - **Potential Relief for Some with IBS:** Following a gluten-free diet may help some people with non-celiac gluten sensitivity feel better about their irritable bowel syndrome (IBS) symptoms.
5. Enhanced Nutrient Absorption:
   - **Improved Nutrient Uptake:** For those with celiac disease, the removal of gluten from the diet aids in the repair of the small intestine's lining, leading to better nutrient absorption. This can help with any dietary shortages brought on by malabsorption.
6. Promotion of Gut Microbiota Balance:
   - **Impact on Gut Microbiota:** The balance of gut bacteria may be positively impacted by a gluten-free diet. Sustaining a thriving microbiological milieu is essential for immune system and general digestive health.
7. Prevention of Cross-Contamination Risks:
   - **Avoidance of Cross-Contamination:** Individuals with gluten sensitivity or celiac disease must be diligent about avoiding cross-contamination. Eliminating gluten from

one's diet also reduces the possibility of unintentional gluten intake leading to symptoms.
8. Potential Reduction in Gastroesophageal Reflux Disease (GERD) Symptoms:
   - **GERD Symptom Management:** After switching to a gluten-free diet, some people with gluten sensitivity may see a decrease in the symptoms of their GERD.
9. Exploration of Alternative Whole Grains:
   - **Diversification of Grain Intake:** A more varied and nutrient-rich diet can be achieved by experimenting with other whole grains, such as quinoa, rice, and gluten-free oats, which are encouraged while following a gluten-free diet.
10. Individualized Dietary Approach:

Tailoring Diet to Personal Needs: Living a gluten-free lifestyle gives people the flexibility to customize their meals to meet their unique requirements, which fosters a feeling of control and personalization in the management of digestive health.

While eating gluten-free has clear health benefits for people with gluten-related problems, maintaining a balanced and nutritionally full diet is crucial for people without specific sensitivity as well. Seeking advice from medical specialists or registered dietitians can help individuals make well-informed dietary decisions that complement their unique needs and health objectives.

- Increased Energy and Mental Clarity

Going gluten-free has been linked to several advantages, including improved mental clarity and higher energy levels, in addition to its well-established effects on digestive health. Although everyone's reaction to a gluten-free diet is different, many people report significant increases in energy and mental clarity. Now let's explore the more subtle ways that avoiding gluten may improve mental clarity and energy:

1. Mitigation of Gluten-Induced Fatigue:
   - **Addressing Gluten-Related Fatigue:** One typical symptom of celiac disease or gluten sensitivity is fatigue. People who avoid gluten-containing meals may feel less fatigued overall, which will boost their energy and give them their vitality back.
2. Stabilization of Blood Sugar Levels:
   - **Impact of Refined Carb content:** A major component of the gluten-free diet is moving away from refined and processed carbs, which are frequently included in goods containing gluten. This dietary adjustment may help to normalize blood sugar levels, which may lessen energy crashes and encourage steady energy production all day.
3. Improved Sleep Quality:
   - **Connections Between Diet and Sleep:** Some people discover that following a gluten-free diet improves the quality of their sleep. People who avoid some of the

inflammatory triggers linked to gluten may sleep better, which will improve their general energy levels and cognitive function when they are awake.
4. Reduction in Brain Fog:
   - **Clarity of Thought:** For many people with gluten sensitivity, brain fog is a subjective sensation that is typified by mental disorientation and difficulties concentrating. Reducing gluten consumption may help to improve mental clarity and function by reducing fog in the brain.
5. Enhanced Cognitive Function:
   - **Positive Influence on Cognitive Abilities:** Going gluten-free has been shown to improve cognitive function in addition to reducing brain fog. Enhancements in memory, focus, and general mental sharpness can lead to an enhanced and concentrated mind.
6. Optimized Nutrient Absorption:
   - **Addressing Nutritional Deficiencies:** Energy levels and cognitive performance may be affected by the inability of celiac disease to absorb essential nutrients. When combined with the right nutritional supplements, a gluten-free diet helps people maximize their absorption of nutrients, which promotes general health.
7. Potential Reduction in Migraines:
   - **Management of Migraine Symptoms:** One well-known symptom of gluten sensitivity in certain people is migraines. A gluten-free diet may help reduce or completely eliminate migraines, which would enhance mental health and quality of life.
8. Individualized Nutrition Plans:
   - **Exploration of Alternative Grains:** People who follow a gluten-free diet are encouraged to try a wide variety of substitute grains, including rice, quinoa, and gluten-free oats. This freedom to choose what to eat makes it possible to create customized nutrition programs that satisfy each person's energy needs and cognitive preferences.
9. Reduced Inflammation:
   - **Systemic Impact of Inflammation:** A number of body systems, including the brain, can be impacted by systemic inflammation, which is a result of gluten sensitivity. Reducing inflammation by gluten elimination may have a good effect on cognitive and mental clarity.
10. Enhanced Mood and Emotional Well-Being:

Addressing Mood Disorders: Anxiety and sadness are among the mood problems that have been associated with gluten sensitivity. A gluten-free diet may help some people experience improvements in their emotional health and mood, which can promote mental health.

It's critical to recognize that not everyone will respond to a gluten-free diet in the same way or get the same health advantages. Additionally, persons without gluten-related diseases should ensure they maintain a balanced and nutritionally complete diet, as eliminating gluten can occasionally lead to nutrient deficits. It is recommended that individuals seeking individualized advice on dietary choices that complement personal health objectives and requirements speak with healthcare experts or certified dietitians.

- Potential Weight Management Benefits

Although celiac illness or gluten sensitivity are the main reasons for going gluten-free, some people also investigate the possibility of weight loss advantages with this dietary strategy. Knowing how a gluten-free diet affects weight will help you understand how this decision may affect your body composition and general wellbeing. Here is a look at some possible advantages of a gluten-free diet for weight loss:

1. Reduction in Caloric Intake:
    - **Focus on Whole, Unprocessed Foods:** Whole, unprocessed foods like fruits, vegetables, lean proteins, and gluten-free grains are frequently highlighted in a gluten-free diet. Goals for weight management may be supported by this change, which can naturally result in a decrease in total caloric consumption.
2. Elimination of Processed Gluten-Containing Foods:
    - **Reduced Intake of Processed Foods:** Refined sugars and harmful fats are other common ingredients in processed foods containing gluten. Giving up these processed foods might result from a gluten-free lifestyle, which would lower the intake of empty calories and help with weight control.
3. Increased Awareness of Food Choices:
    - **Mindful Eating Habits:** Making a conscious effort to avoid gluten might increase one's awareness of what they consume and encourage mindful eating. A more aware approach to nutrition and portion control may result from this mindfulness.
4. Potential Reduction in Bloating and Water Retention:
    - **Alleviation of Digestive Discomfort:** Eliminating gluten can help those with celiac disease or gluten sensitivity who experience gastrointestinal pain by reducing bloating and water retention. This decrease in discomfort may help people perceive that they are managing their weight even though it is not a sign of fat loss.
5. Exploration of Alternative Grains:
    - **Incorporation of Nutrient-Rich Alternatives:** Investigating substitute grains like quinoa, brown rice, and gluten-free oats is a common step in a gluten-free diet. Higher nutritional content from these grains, including fiber and other nutrients, can help with satiety and weight management.
6. Balanced Macronutrient Profile:
    - **Focus on Balanced Nutrition:** People who follow a gluten-free diet might focus more on reaching a balanced macronutrient profile, which consists of a variety of healthy

fats, proteins, and carbohydrates. This well-rounded strategy can help with weight control and general wellness.
7. Potential Improvement in Insulin Sensitivity:
   - **Impact on Insulin Levels:** A gluten-free diet may help people with disorders like non-celiac gluten sensitivity by improving their insulin sensitivity, according to some research. Higher insulin sensitivity is linked to better blood sugar regulation and may help with weight loss.
8. Individualized Nutritional Strategies:
   - **Tailoring Nutrition to Personal Needs:** Adopting a gluten-free diet enables customized eating plans. This adaptability can result in a more customized eating strategy that fits individual dietary preferences and maximizes nutritional intake for weight-related objectives.
9. Focus on Lean Proteins and Vegetables:
   - **Emphasis on Lean Protein Sources:** Lean proteins and vegetables are frequently the focus of a gluten-free diet, encouraging the consumption of nutrient-dense, low-calorie foods that help with feelings of fullness and pleasure..
10. Potential for Improved Digestive Efficiency:

Enhanced Digestive Function: Eliminating gluten can enhance digestive efficiency in those with celiac disease or gluten sensitivity. This could lead to a more efficient use of nutrients, which could have an effect on general health and weight control.

It's important to remember that not everyone will lose weight as a result of a gluten-free diet because the effect on weight control is quite specific. People should also be aware of the importance of eating a balanced, nutritionally full diet because cutting out gluten can occasionally result in nutrient shortages. It is recommended that individuals seeking individualized advice on dietary choices that complement personal health objectives and requirements speak with healthcare experts or certified dietitians.

Chapter 2
Navigating the Gluten-Free Pantry

- Essential Gluten-Free Ingredients: Gluten-Free Flours and Starches

It's new to choose flours and starches in a gluten-free kitchen because traditional wheat flours are off limits. Embracing a variety of gluten-free alternatives ensures that your culinary endeavors turn out well and gives you access to a wide variety of delectable flavors. Now let's look at the main gluten-free flours and starches that will enhance your baking and culinary efforts:

1. Almond Flour:
   - **Overview:** Almond flour, made from finely ground almonds, is a nutrient-rich gluten-free alternative.
   - **Application:** Ideal for baking, almond flour adds a moist, nutty flavor to baked goods such as cookies, cakes, and muffins.
   - **Considerations:** Almond flour's high fat content can impact texture, so it's often used in combination with other flours.
2. Coconut Flour:
   - **Overview:** Coconut flour, derived from dried coconut meat, is a high-fiber, low-carb option.
   - **Application:** Suitable for both sweet and savory dishes, coconut flour adds a subtle coconut flavor and helps absorb moisture in recipes.
   - **Considerations:** It has a unique texture, and recipes often require additional liquid to balance its absorbent nature.
3. Brown Rice Flour:
   - **Overview:** Ground from brown rice, this flour offers a mild, slightly nutty taste.
   - **Application:** A versatile choice for both baking and cooking, brown rice flour works well in bread, cookies, and as a coating for fried foods.
   - **Considerations:** It can be dense, so blending with lighter flours is common for optimal results.
4. Quinoa Flour:
   - **Overview:** Quinoa flour, made from ground quinoa seeds, is a protein-rich option.
   - **Application:** Suitable for a variety of recipes, including pancakes, cookies, and bread, quinoa flour adds a wholesome element and boosts protein content.
   - **Considerations:** Its distinct flavor may require complementary ingredients for a balanced taste.
5. Oat Flour (Certified Gluten-Free):
   - **Overview:** Oat flour, processed from certified gluten-free oats, offers a mild and slightly sweet flavor.

- **Application:** Ideal for baking, oat flour contributes a soft, moist texture to products like muffins, pancakes, and quick breads.
- **Considerations:** Ensure it's labeled gluten-free to avoid cross-contamination with wheat.

6. Tapioca Starch/Flour:
   - **Overview:** Tapioca flour, extracted from the cassava root, provides a light and airy texture.
   - **Application:** Commonly used in combination with other flours, tapioca flour enhances the elasticity and chewiness of baked goods.
   - **Considerations:** Use in moderation, as excessive tapioca flour can result in a gummy texture.

7. Potato Starch:
   - **Overview:** Extracted from potatoes, this starch is a versatile addition to gluten-free cooking.
   - **Application:** Potato starch contributes to the lightness of baked goods and is often used in conjunction with other flours for optimal results.
   - **Considerations:** It has a neutral flavor and works well in recipes where a light texture is desired.

8. Cornstarch:
   - **Overview:** Cornstarch, derived from corn kernels, is a common thickening agent.
   - **Application:** Primarily used as a thickener in sauces, gravies, and desserts, cornstarch provides a silky texture.
   - **Considerations:** While not a flour, cornstarch is gluten-free and plays a crucial role in gluten-free cooking.

9. Sorghum Flour:
   - **Overview:** Ground from sorghum grain, this flour has a mild, slightly sweet taste.
   - **Application:** A versatile option for baking, sorghum flour works well in a variety of recipes, including cookies, cakes, and bread.
   - **Considerations:** It's a good source of fiber and nutrients, adding nutritional value to your gluten-free creations.

10. Chickpea Flour (Garbanzo Bean Flour):
    - **Overview:** Made from ground chickpeas, this flour offers a distinctive, slightly nutty flavor.
    - **Application:** Chickpea flour is versatile, suitable for savory dishes like socca (a type of flatbread) and as a binding agent in recipes like veggie burgers.
    - **Considerations:** Its strong flavor may influence the taste of the final dish.

The best outcomes when dealing with gluten-free flours and starches are frequently achieved via experimentation and a willingness to combine diverse choices. Make your selections according to the taste and texture you prefer for a certain recipe, and don't be afraid to combine different types of flour to achieve a well-rounded and fulfilling result. In some recipes, you may also want to try using gums like guar gum or xanthan gum to simulate the binding qualities of gluten.

- Whole Grains Without Gluten

Giving up gluten doesn't have to mean giving up on whole grains' healthy goodness and nutritional advantages. A wide variety of gluten-free whole grains are available that not only support those with celiac disease or gluten sensitivity but also add vital nutrients to a diet that is well-balanced. Let's investigate this nutrient-dense, gluten-free world of whole grains:

1. Quinoa:
   - **Nutritional Profile:** A complete protein source, quinoa is rich in fiber, vitamins (such as B vitamins), and minerals (including iron and magnesium).
   - **Usage:** Use quinoa as a base for salads, pilafs, or as a gluten-free alternative to traditional grains in various recipes.
2. Brown Rice:
   - **Nutritional Profile:** A good source of complex carbohydrates, brown rice contains fiber, B vitamins, and minerals like manganese.
   - **Usage:** Incorporate brown rice into side dishes, casseroles, or use it as a base for stir-fries and pilafs.
3. Wild Rice:
   - **Nutritional Profile:** Packed with antioxidants, fiber, and protein, wild rice offers a nutrient-dense alternative.
   - **Usage:** Combine wild rice with vegetables, nuts, and herbs for hearty salads or use it as a side dish.
4. Amaranth:
   - **Nutritional Profile:** High in protein and fiber, amaranth provides essential amino acids, iron, and calcium.
   - **Usage:** Cook amaranth as a hot cereal, blend it into soups, or use it in gluten-free baked goods for added nutrition.
5. Millet:
   - **Nutritional Profile:** Millet is a good source of magnesium, phosphorus, and antioxidants.
   - **Usage:** Cook millet as a side dish, use it in porridge, or incorporate it into gluten-free baking for a delicate, slightly sweet flavor.
6. Buckwheat:
   - **Nutritional Profile:** Despite its name, buckwheat is not wheat and is gluten-free. It provides protein, fiber, and essential minerals like manganese.
   - **Usage:** Enjoy buckwheat in pancakes, porridge, or as a substitute for traditional grains in various dishes.

7. Sorghum:
   - **Nutritional Profile:** Sorghum is rich in fiber, antioxidants, and provides vitamins and minerals, including iron and magnesium.
   - **Usage:** Use sorghum flour in baking or cook whole sorghum grains as a nutritious base for salads and pilafs.
8. Teff:
   - **Nutritional Profile:** Teff is a gluten-free ancient grain rich in iron, calcium, and protein.
   - **Usage:** Cook teff as a porridge, use it as a base for stews, or incorporate teff flour into gluten-free baking for a nutty flavor.
9. Gluten-Free Oats:
   - **Nutritional Profile:** Oats are a good source of fiber, vitamins, and minerals, particularly beta-glucans that support heart health.
   - **Usage:** Enjoy gluten-free oats as oatmeal, use them in baking, or blend them into smoothies for added nutrition.
10. Sorghum:
    - **Nutritional Profile:** Sorghum is rich in fiber, antioxidants, and provides vitamins and minerals, including iron and magnesium.
    - **Usage:** Use sorghum flour in baking or cook whole sorghum grains as a nutritious base for salads and pilafs.
11. Teff:
    - **Nutritional Profile:** Teff is a gluten-free ancient grain rich in iron, calcium, and protein.
    - **Usage:** Cook teff as a porridge, use it as a base for stews, or incorporate teff flour into gluten-free baking for a nutty flavor.
12. Gluten-Free Oats:
    - **Nutritional Profile:** Oats are a good source of fiber, vitamins, and minerals, particularly beta-glucans that support heart health.
    - **Usage:** Enjoy gluten-free oats as oatmeal, use them in baking, or blend them into smoothies for added nutrition.
13. Buckwheat:
    - **Nutritional Profile:** Despite its name, buckwheat is not wheat and is gluten-free. It provides protein, fiber, and essential minerals like manganese.
    - **Usage:** Enjoy buckwheat in pancakes, porridge, or as a substitute for traditional grains in various dishes.
14. Sorghum:
    - **Nutritional Profile:** Sorghum is rich in fiber, antioxidants, and provides vitamins and minerals, including iron and magnesium.
    - **Usage:** Use sorghum flour in baking or cook whole sorghum grains as a nutritious base for salads and pilafs.

15. Teff:
    - **Nutritional Profile:** Teff is a gluten-free ancient grain rich in iron, calcium, and protein.
    - **Usage:** Cook teff as a porridge, use it as a base for stews, or incorporate teff flour into gluten-free baking for a nutty flavor.
16. Gluten-Free Oats:
    - **Nutritional Profile:** Oats are a good source of fiber, vitamins, and minerals, particularly beta-glucans that support heart health.
    - **Usage:** Enjoy gluten-free oats as oatmeal, use them in baking, or blend them into smoothies for added nutrition.

Each of these gluten-free whole grains brings its unique nutritional profile and culinary versatility to the table. Experimenting with these grains allows for the creation of diverse, flavorful dishes that not only cater to dietary restrictions but also contribute to a well-rounded and nourishing diet. Whether in hot cereals, salads, pilafs, or baked goods, these gluten-free whole grains offer a wide range of options for those seeking a nutrient-rich and delicious approach to gluten-free living.

- Gluten-Free Binders and Thickeners

Binders and thickeners are frequently needed in gluten-free recipes to preserve the desired texture and consistency. These components are essential for simulating the structural qualities of gluten and giving different foods stability, moisture retention, and structure. Examine these binders and thickeners without gluten to improve the caliber of your dishes:

1. Xanthan Gum:
    - **Function:** A versatile and widely used gluten-free binder and thickener.
    - **Application:** Adds elasticity to dough, enhances texture in baked goods, and prevents ingredient separation in liquids.
    - **Considerations:** Use in small amounts, as excess xanthan gum can result in a gummy texture.
2. Guar Gum:
    - **Function:** Similar to xanthan gum, guar gum is a natural thickening agent.
    - **Application:** Commonly used in gluten-free baking to improve texture and structure in bread and other baked goods.
    - **Considerations:** It may be more suitable for those with sensitivities to other gums.
3. Psyllium Husk Powder:
    - **Function:** Acts as a binding agent and adds structure to gluten-free dough.
    - **Application:** Particularly effective in gluten-free bread recipes, providing a moist and springy texture.

- **Considerations:** Ensure proper hydration, as psyllium husk absorbs a significant amount of liquid.
4. Chia Seeds:
    - **Function:** Chia seeds, when mixed with water, form a gel-like substance, acting as a binding agent.
    - **Application:** Use as an egg substitute in baking or incorporate into recipes for added texture and nutritional benefits.
    - **Considerations:** Allow the mixture to sit for a few minutes to achieve the desired gel-like consistency.
5. Flaxseed Meal:
    - **Function:** Similar to chia seeds, flaxseed meal can be used as an egg replacement and binder.
    - **Application:** Ideal for adding moisture and structure to gluten-free baked goods.
    - **Considerations:** Combine with water and let it rest to develop a gel-like consistency before incorporating into recipes.
6. Arrowroot Powder:
    - **Function:** A gluten-free thickening agent with a neutral taste.
    - **Application:** Suitable for sauces, gravies, and fruit fillings, providing a glossy finish.
    - **Considerations:** Mix arrowroot powder with a cold liquid before adding it to hot mixtures to prevent clumping.
7. Cornstarch:
    - **Function:** A classic thickener derived from corn.
    - **Application:** Widely used in both sweet and savory recipes, such as soups, sauces, and pie fillings.
    - **Considerations:** Mix with a small amount of cold liquid before adding to hot mixtures to avoid lumps.
8. Potato Starch:
    - **Function:** Adds thickness and moisture to gluten-free recipes.
    - **Application:** Commonly used in baking to enhance the texture of bread and other baked goods.
    - **Considerations:** Ideal for recipes where a lighter texture is desired.
9. Tapioca Starch/Flour:
    - **Function:** A versatile thickener with a mild flavor.
    - **Application:** Adds chewiness to gluten-free bread and enhances the texture in various baked goods.
    - **Considerations:** Use in combination with other flours for optimal results in baking.
10. Gelatin:
    - **Function:** Acts as a setting agent and thickener, particularly in desserts.
    - **Application:** Use in recipes such as puddings, mousses, and gummy candies.
    - **Considerations:** Requires hydration in liquid before incorporating into recipes.

11. Agar-Agar:
    - **Function:** A plant-based alternative to gelatin, agar-agar sets and thickens.
    - **Application:** Suitable for jellies, custards, and vegan desserts.
    - **Considerations:** Activate by simmering in liquid, and it sets at room temperature.
12. Rice Flour Slurry:
    - **Function:** Rice flour mixed with water creates a slurry that acts as a thickening agent.
    - **Application:** Use in sauces, gravies, and soups to achieve the desired consistency.

Considerations: To avoid clumping, combine rice flour with cold liquid before adding it to hot mixes.

You may adjust recipes to your diet and tastes by experimenting with these gluten-free thickeners and binders. Keep in mind that the appropriate combination may vary depending on the exact dish you're cooking, so don't hesitate to explore and find the perfect balance for your gluten-free culinary creations.

- Substituting Gluten in Common Recipes: Adapting Traditional Recipes to Be Gluten-Free

Making traditional meals gluten-free needs careful consideration of the ingredients you use and how you prepare them. Take on the challenge head-on as you make your way through the world of gluten-free cookery. This is a how-to on replacing gluten in popular recipes so that your food still tastes, feels, and is satisfyingly high:

1. All-Purpose Gluten-Free Flour Blends:
    - **Overview:** Commercial or homemade gluten-free flour blends mimic the versatility of all-purpose wheat flour.
    - **Application:** Substitute gluten-free flour blends cupful-for-cupful in recipes for cookies, muffins, and pancakes.
    - **Considerations:** Choose blends with a mix of flours like rice, sorghum, and starches for optimal results.
2. Almond Flour:
    - **Overview:** Ground almonds create a rich, moist texture in baked goods.
    - **Application:** Ideal for recipes like almond flour pancakes, almond meal cookies, or almond-crusted proteins.
    - **Considerations:** Adjust the liquid content in recipes, as almond flour can be denser than wheat flour.
3. Coconut Flour:
    - **Overview:** Derived from dried coconut, coconut flour adds a subtle tropical flavor.
    - **Application:** Use in gluten-free baking for recipes like coconut flour bread, muffins, and cakes.

- **Considerations:** Coconut flour is highly absorbent; ensure adequate liquid and consider blending with other flours.
4. Oat Flour (Certified Gluten-Free):
   - **Overview:** Ground gluten-free oats provide a mild, slightly nutty flavor.
   - **Application:** Substitute for wheat flour in recipes like oat flour pancakes, cookies, and quick breads.
   - **Considerations:** Choose certified gluten-free oats to avoid cross-contamination.
5. Quinoa Flour:
   - **Overview:** Ground quinoa seeds offer a protein-rich, nutty alternative.
   - **Application:** Incorporate into gluten-free recipes for quinoa flour pizza crust, muffins, or flatbreads.
   - **Considerations:** Experiment with blending quinoa flour with other flours for balanced flavor and texture.
6. Brown Rice Flour:
   - **Overview:** Milled from brown rice, this flour has a neutral taste.
   - **Application:** Use in recipes like brown rice flour cookies, bread, and as a coating for fried foods.
   - **Considerations:** Combine with starches for improved texture and structure.
7. Tapioca Starch/Flour:
   - **Overview:** Extracted from the cassava root, tapioca starch adds lightness.
   - **Application:** Combine with other flours in recipes for tapioca flour tortillas, pies, and dumplings.
   - **Considerations:** Use in moderation, as excessive tapioca flour can result in a gummy texture.
8. Potato Starch:
   - **Overview:** A versatile starch that contributes to the fluffiness of baked goods.
   - **Application:** Use in recipes for potato starch pancakes, gluten-free bread, and as a thickener in sauces.
   - **Considerations:** Combine with other flours for optimal results in baking.
9. Chickpea Flour (Garbanzo Bean Flour):
   - **Overview:** Ground chickpeas provide a hearty, nutty flavor.
   - **Application:** Incorporate into recipes for chickpea flour flatbreads, fritters, and savory pancakes.
   - **Considerations:** Experiment with complementary flavors to balance the strong taste.
10. Sorghum Flour:
    - **Overview:** Milled from sorghum grain, this flour offers a mild, slightly sweet taste.
    - **Application:** Substitute for wheat flour in recipes like sorghum flour muffins, cookies, and cakes.
    - **Considerations:** Blend with other flours for a well-rounded flavor profile.

Recall that in order to get the right texture and flavor, successful gluten-free adaptations frequently need experimenting with different flour blends. To build your own unique flour blend, don't be scared to mix different gluten-free flours and starches together. In addition, think about using binders, such as guar gum or xanthan gum, to simulate the elasticity of gluten in specific recipes. You may become an expert in gluten-free cooking and discover a world of delectable options if you have patience and inventiveness.

- Understanding the Role of Xanthan Gum and Guar Gum

Guar gum and xanthan gum serve as vital thickeners and binders in gluten-free cooking, making them invaluable tools. These all-natural components are essential to the success of a variety of gluten-free recipes since they replicate the cohesive qualities of gluten. Now let's examine the differences between xanthan gum and guar gum and their uses:

1. Xanthan Gum:
    - **Source:** Produced through the fermentation of sugar by the Xanthomonas campestris bacterium.
    - **Texture and Consistency:** Xanthan gum forms a viscous, gel-like substance when combined with liquids, creating a flexible structure similar to gluten.
    - Applications:
        - **Baking:** Enhances the elasticity and moisture retention in gluten-free bread, cakes, and cookies.
        - **Sauces and Dressings:** Acts as a thickening agent, preventing separation and providing a smooth, consistent texture.
        - **Ice Cream:** Improves the creaminess and prevents ice crystals from forming.
2. Guar Gum:
    - **Source:** Extracted from guar beans (Cyamopsis tetragonoloba).
    - **Texture and Consistency:** Guar gum forms a gel when hydrated, contributing to the viscosity and binding properties in recipes.
    - Applications:
        - **Baking:** Adds structure and elasticity to gluten-free baked goods, including bread, muffins, and pancakes.
        - **Dairy and Non-Dairy Products:** Stabilizes the texture of yogurts, kefir, and plant-based milk alternatives.
        - **Sauces and Soups:** Acts as a thickening agent in gravies, sauces, and soups, creating a smooth and consistent texture.

Considerations When Using Xanthan Gum and Guar Gum:

1. Quantity:

- **Start Small:** Begin with a minimal amount of xanthan gum or guar gum, especially in baking, as a little goes a long way.
- **Adjust to Taste:** Gradually increase the quantity based on the desired texture and consistency of the final dish.
2. Combining Gums:
   - **Synergistic Effects:** In some recipes, a combination of xanthan gum and guar gum may yield superior results, offering a balanced texture.
   - **Experimentation:** Explore different ratios of xanthan gum to guar gum to find the ideal combination for specific recipes.
3. Hydration:
   - **Hydrate Properly:** Both xanthan gum and guar gum require proper hydration to function effectively.
   - **Mixing Technique:** Blend the gum with other dry ingredients before adding liquids to ensure even distribution and prevent clumping.
4. Recipe Adaptations:
   - **Versatility:** In recipes, xanthan gum and guar gum can be used interchangeably; however, the best option may vary depending on the particular qualities required.
   - **Recipe Modification:** Adapt traditional recipes to be gluten-free by incorporating xanthan gum or guar gum to achieve the desired structure.
5. Texture Preferences:
   - **Personal Taste:** Try varying the amount of xanthan gum or guar gum to suit your own texture preferences, such as a light and soft cake or a chewy bread.
6. Storage:
   - **Seal Properly:** Store xanthan gum and guar gum in airtight containers to prevent moisture absorption, which can affect their performance.
   - **Cool and Dark:** Keep these gums in a cool, dark place to maintain their quality over time.

Knowing the differences between guar gum and xanthan gum allows you to confidently handle the subtleties of gluten-free cuisine. Whether you're creating a gluten-free bread recipe or thickening a savory sauce, these kitchen necessities play a critical part in achieving the desired texture and consistency in a variety of culinary masterpieces.

- Tips for Successful Gluten-Free Baking

Although baking without gluten presents its own set of difficulties, you may still produce mouthwatering and fulfilling desserts if you have the necessary skills and expertise. The following are crucial pointers to help you succeed in your gluten-free baking:

1. Select High-Quality Gluten-Free Flours:

- **Diverse Blends:** Try different combinations of rice flour, sorghum flour, tapioca starch, and potato starch to achieve the best possible texture and flavor when making gluten-free flour mixes.
- **Certified Gluten-Free:** Select gluten-free flours with certification to avoid cross-contamination and guarantee ingredient integrity.

2. Understand the Role of Binders:
   - **Xanthan Gum or Guar Gum:** Use these binders to replicate the gluten's flexibility. Start with tiny amounts and adjust according to the requirements of the dish.

3. Balance Liquid and Dry Ingredients:
   - **Hydration:** Compared to regular flours, gluten-free flours frequently need more liquid. To create a well-balanced batter or dough, adjust the proportions of moist to dry elements.
   - **Texture Check:** The consistency should resemble thick cake batter or soft cookie dough.

4. Add Moisture-Retaining Ingredients:
   - **Fruits and Vegetables:** Include ingredients like applesauce, mashed bananas, or grated zucchini to add moisture and enhance texture.
   - **Greek Yogurt or Sour Cream:** These dairy products contribute richness and moisture to baked goods.

5. Incorporate Nut and Seed Flours:
   - **Almond, Coconut, or Hazelnut Flour:** Introduce nut and seed flours for a nutty flavor and added moisture. Adjust the ratio to balance texture.

6. Prevent Grittiness with Rice Flour:
   - **Fine Texture:** Opt for finely ground rice flour to minimize grittiness in your baked goods. A combination of rice flour and starches often works well.

7. Experiment with Alternative Sweeteners:
   - **Honey, Maple Syrup, or Agave Nectar:** Explore natural sweeteners to add depth to your treats. Adjust the quantity based on sweetness preferences.

8. Use Room Temperature Ingredients:
   - **Butter and Eggs:** Allow butter and eggs to reach room temperature before incorporating them into the batter. This enhances the blending process and promotes a smoother texture.

9. Let the Batter Rest:
   - **Resting Time:** Allow the batter or dough to rest before baking to hydrate the flours fully. This improves the final texture and structure.

10. Monitor Baking Times:
    - **Temperature Adjustment:** To prevent overbrowning, baked foods free of gluten might need to be baked at a slightly lower temperature. Keep a watchful eye on things to avoid drying out.

11. Experiment with Flour Combinations:

- **Blend Varieties:** To achieve a harmony of flavors and textures, blend various gluten-free flours. For a complimentary mixture, try combining rice flour with almond flour, for instance.
12. Mindful Mixing Techniques:
    - **Gentle Folding:** Mix ingredients gently to avoid overworking the batter. This prevents the development of a dense texture.
13. Invest in Quality Baking Pans:
    - **Non-Stick Surfaces:** To avoid sticking, use baking pans that are non-stick or line them with parchment paper. This makes removing your baked items simple.
14. Cool Thoroughly Before Slicing:
    - **Patience Pays Off:** Allow gluten-free baked goods to cool completely before slicing. This helps them set and improves the texture.
15. Store Properly for Freshness:

Airtight Containers: To keep your creations fresh and avoid drying them out, store them in airtight containers.

Using these pointers, you'll be ready to start baking with gluten substitutes and create delicious desserts that are just as tasty and texture-worthy as their conventional counterparts. Recall that finding the ideal ratio of components and methods for your gluten-free products will require patience and trial.

- Reading Labels Like a Pro: Identifying Hidden Sources of Gluten

It's important for people who follow a gluten-free diet to read food labels. While many components are clearly known to contain gluten, others could go by alternative labels. Here's how to expertly read labels:

1. Identify Common Gluten-Containing Ingredients:
   - Gluten is evident in wheat, barley, rye, and their derivatives.
   - Keep an eye out for less evident sources such as brewer's yeast, malt, malt extract, and flavoring.
2. Gluten-Free Certification Symbols:
   - Trust items with recognized gluten-free certification insignia, such as the Gluten-Free Certification Organization (GFCO) or the Certified Gluten-Free label from the Gluten Intolerance Group.
3. Check for Cross-Contamination Warnings:
   - Statements such as "produced at a facility that also processes wheat" or "may contain wheat" are frequently included by manufacturers. If you suffer from celiac disease or extreme gluten sensitivity, heed these recommendations with caution.

4. Look for Naturally Gluten-Free Foods:
   - Natural gluten-free foods include fruits, vegetables, meats, dairy products, and other whole, unprocessed foods. On the other hand, be cautious when processing or preparing to avoid cross-contamination.
5. Study Ingredient Lists:
   - Analyze ingredient lists for hidden gluten sources, including modified food starch, hydrolyzed vegetable protein, and certain food colorings.
6. Understand Codex Alimentarius Wheat Starch:
   - Certain areas classify wheat starch with the "Codex Alimentarius" mark as gluten-free. It is imperative to ascertain one's tolerance threshold and seek advice from a healthcare provider.
7. Be Cautious with Oats:
   - Oats are naturally gluten-free, but during processing, cross-contamination occurs frequently. Choose gluten-free oats that have been certified to exceed stringent purity requirements.

Gluten-Free Certification and Labeling

1. Certification Organizations:
   - Familiarize yourself with reputable gluten-free certification organizations, including GFCO, NSF Gluten-Free, and the Gluten-Free Certification Program (GFCP).
2. Certification Symbols:
   - Look for distinct symbols on packaging that indicate gluten-free certification. These symbols provide assurance that the product has undergone rigorous testing.
3. Cross-Contact Protocols:
   - Certified products adhere to strict cross-contact prevention protocols, reducing the risk of gluten contamination during manufacturing.
4. Online Certification Directories:
   - Utilize online directories provided by certification organizations to verify the gluten-free status of specific products.

Navigating Ambiguous Ingredients Lists

1. Educate Yourself on Alternate Names for Gluten:
   - Learn the various names for gluten-containing ingredients, such as durum, semolina, and farina, to better identify them on labels.
2. Watch for Hidden Sources:
   - Be vigilant for hidden gluten in additives like maltodextrin, modified food starch, and flavorings, which may be derived from gluten-containing grains.
3. Question Ambiguous Terms:

- For more information, get in touch with the manufacturer if an ingredient appears confusing or unclear. A lot of businesses are eager to give comprehensive product details.
4. Use Gluten-Free Apps and Resources:
   - Leverage gluten-free apps and online resources that offer databases of safe and unsafe ingredients, helping you make informed choices while shopping.
5. Stay Informed About Labeling Laws:
   - Keep abreast on local labeling rules and requirements. You can trust the information on food labels if you are aware of these laws.
6. Choose Certified Gluten-Free Products:

Choose goods that are clearly certified gluten-free wherever feasible. This extra level of examination gives greater confidence.

By honing your label-reading abilities, comprehending gluten-free certifications, and navigating ambiguous ingredients lists with confidence, you empower yourself to make informed choices in harmony with your gluten-free lifestyle.

Chapter 3
Setting the Foundation

- Organizing Your Gluten-Free Workspace

A flawless cooking experience requires setting up a clean, gluten-free environment. To create a productive and secure atmosphere, take the following actions:

1. Designate Gluten-Free Zones:
   - Establish specific areas in your kitchen as gluten-free zones. Designate countertops, utensils, and appliances exclusively for gluten-free food preparation.
2. Separate Gluten-Free and Gluten-Containing Ingredients:
   - Store gluten-free ingredients separately from gluten-containing ones. Use dedicated cabinets, shelves, or storage containers to prevent cross-contamination.
3. Label Clearly:
   - Clearly label gluten-free products and containers to avoid confusion. Use color-coded labels or a dedicated section in your pantry for easy identification.
4. Invest in Gluten-Free Kitchen Tools:
   - Purchase a separate set of kitchen tools, cutting boards, and utensils designated for gluten-free cooking. This reduces the risk of cross-contact during food preparation.
5. Use Color-Coded Utensils:
   - Employ a color-coded system for utensils to distinguish between those used for gluten-free and gluten-containing ingredients. For example, choose red for gluten-free and blue for gluten-containing.
6. Implement Separate Cookware:
   - Use distinct cookware for gluten-free cooking. Consider investing in stainless steel, glass, or cast iron pans that are easier to clean and less likely to retain gluten residues.
7. Dedicate Toaster and Appliances:
   - Reserve a separate toaster, blender, and other small appliances for gluten-free items. Crumbs from gluten-containing products can linger in appliances and pose a risk.
8. Organize Pantry and Refrigerator:
   - Organize your fridge and pantry so that gluten-free foods are always close at hand. To avoid unintentional cross-contamination, group comparable products together and position gluten-free items on higher shelves.
9. Establish Gluten-Free Meal Prep Area:
   - Create a designated area for meal prep, ensuring it's exclusively used for gluten-free food assembly. This can be a separate section of your countertop or a dedicated table.
10. Regularly Clean and Sanitize:

- To get rid of any possible gluten remains, follow a comprehensive cleaning regimen. Regularly sterilize surfaces, utensils, and appliances to maintain a safe and hygienic workspace.
11. Educate Household Members:
    - Make sure that everyone in your home is aware of how crucial it is to keep gluten-free areas intact. Teach family members the importance of staying in specified locations and the dangers of cross-contamination.
12. Review Labels Before Purchase:
    - Develop a habit of carefully reading labels before purchasing new products. This practice helps you make informed decisions and ensures that any new additions to your kitchen are gluten-free.
13. Establish Clear Communication:
    - Tell everybody who shares your kitchen that you must be gluten-free. Promote candid discussion regarding the significance of preserving the integrity of gluten-free areas.
14. Consider Dedicated Gluten-Free Storage Containers:

To avoid confusion, store gluten-free leftovers in different containers. Label containers clearly to indicate which contents are gluten-free and which contain gluten.

By putting these tips into practice, you can establish a neat, cross-contamination-free workspace that promotes a secure and pleasurable cooking environment. You must be meticulous and consistent if you want to keep your gluten-free kitchen looking its best.

- Essential Kitchen Tools and Appliances

It's critical to stock your kitchen with the appropriate cookware and gadgets in order to prepare tasty and secure gluten-free meals. Whether you're a seasoned gluten-free cook or you're just getting started, having the right tools guarantees accuracy, speed, and enjoyment in the kitchen. Let's examine each crucial item in more detail:

1. Dedicated Gluten-Free Utensils:
    - Think about utilizing cutlery from a different set that is just meant to be used for gluten-free cooking, or cutlery that is color-coded. By doing this, the possibility of cross-contamination is decreased, protecting those who are gluten sensitive.
2. Gluten-Free Cutting Boards:
    - Invest in cutting boards that are specifically meant for preparing gluten-free meals, made of non-porous materials like glass or plastic. Select cutting boards that are simple to sterilize and clean in order to keep your workspace gluten-free.
3. High-Quality Chef's Knife:

- A good, sharp chef's knife is a multipurpose kitchen tool that's necessary for precisely chopping veggies, slicing meats, and making gluten-free recipes. Make sure you sharpen it frequently to keep it working well.

4. Mixing Bowls:
   - Assemble a set of mixing bowls in varying sizes to handle a range of culinary duties. Mixing bowls come be handy for a variety of tasks, from arranging colorful salads to whisking ingredients for gluten-free recipes.

5. Whisks and Mixing Spoons:
   - To make recipes smooth and well-blended, whisks and mixing spoons are essential. These tools guarantee consistent results when making gluten-free dressings, batters, or sauces.

6. Measuring Cupful and Spoons:
   - Accurate measurements are crucial in gluten-free baking. Invest in durable and precise measuring cupful and spoons to ensure the proper balance of ingredients in your gluten-free recipes.

7. Food Processor:
   - Food processors make making gluten-free meals more efficient by slicing, chopping, and mixing items with ease. Use it to make nut butters, delicious sauces, and flours free of gluten.

8. Blender:
   - A good blender is a useful tool for cooking without gluten. A blender is an essential kitchen appliance that can be used for creating healthy smoothies and making gluten-free soups.

9. Stand Mixer:
   - Blending dough and recipes free of gluten is made easier with a stand mixer. Select attachments that meet the requirements of gluten-free baking, such as dough hooks for kneading and paddle attachments for mixing.

10. Rolling Pin:
    - When rolling out gluten-free dough, use a rolling pin made of materials like marble or stainless steel to provide a clean, smooth surface. Cross-contact is avoided by using specialized rolling pins.

11. Baking Sheets and Pans:
    - Build a collection of gluten-free baking sheets, cake pans, and muffin tins with non-stick surfaces for easy release. Consider materials that distribute heat evenly for consistent baking results.

12. Silicone Baking Mats:
    - The best way to stop gluten-free baked items from sticking to pans is to use silicone baking mats. These mats encourage level baking and simplify cleanup, making them an excellent addition to your kitchen.

13. Cooling Racks:

- When it comes to preserving the texture of gluten-free baked goods, cooling racks are essential. Raising them ensures a nice consistency and prevents sogginess by allowing air to circulate evenly.

14. Dedicated Toaster:
    - To prevent cross-contamination, invest in a separate toaster exclusively for gluten-free bread and other gluten-free items. This eliminates the risk of gluten residues transferring to your gluten-free snacks.

15. Gluten-Free Bread Machine:
    - A gluten-free bread machine simplifies the process of creating tasty gluten-free bread. For individualized results, look for models with customizable crust options and gluten-free settings.

16. Sifter:
    - A sifter is a valuable tool for incorporating air into gluten-free flours, preventing lumps and ensuring a light and airy texture in your gluten-free baked goods.

17. Parchment Paper and Aluminum Foil:
    - When cooking without gluten, parchment paper is a useful ally since it keeps food from adhering and encourages quick release. When roasting gluten-free foods, aluminum foil helps to ensure even cooking.

18. Kitchen Scale:
    - Accurate measurements are paramount in gluten-free baking. Invest in a kitchen scale to precisely measure ingredients, ensuring consistency and perfecting your gluten-free recipes.

19. Instant-Read Thermometer:
    - A useful tool for measuring the internal temperature of baked items, including gluten-free bread, is an instant-read thermometer. By doing this, you can be sure they're cooked through without losing any moisture.

20. Food Storage Containers:
    - Keep a variety of airtight jars on hand to store grains, gluten-free flours, and leftovers. To avoid confusion and guarantee the freshness of your gluten-free foods, carefully label your containers.

21. Gluten-Free Cookbook or Recipe Binder:
    - Arrange your best gluten-free recipes into a binder or cookbook that is specifically designed for this purpose. This customized tool becomes a go-to source for cooking delectable meals.

22. Label Maker:

To identify clearly which objects, containers, and areas in your kitchen are gluten-free, use a label maker. This easy-to-use organizing solution lowers the chance of unintentional gluten exposure while increasing efficiency.

You may not only create a safe and comfortable atmosphere for people with gluten sensitivities by carefully choosing and keeping these necessary tools and appliances, but you're also laying the groundwork for successful gluten-free cooking. Everything on this extensive list is essential to making your gluten-free cooking efforts go more smoothly.

- Creating a Meal Plan for Success

Developing a thoughtful food plan is essential to adjusting to a gluten-free diet. A well-thought-out meal plan reduces anxiety during mealtimes while also guaranteeing balanced nourishment. Now let's explore the processes and factors to take into account while making a gluten-free meal plan that prepares you for a successful and fulfilling culinary adventure:

1. Assess Dietary Needs and Preferences:
    - Assessing your nutritional requirements, preferences, and any particular health concerns should come first. Find gluten-free substitutes for your favorite dishes to ensure a smooth transition.
2. Build a Foundation with Whole Foods:
    - Give top priority to entire, naturally gluten-free foods including dairy, quinoa, rice, and vegetables as well as lean meats and fruits. These are the cornerstones of a varied and wholesome gluten-free diet.
3. Plan Balanced Meals:
    - Ensure each meal incorporates a balance of macronutrients—proteins, carbohydrates, and fats. Include a variety of colorful fruits and vegetables to maximize nutrient intake.
4. Explore Gluten-Free Recipe Resources:
    - Use gluten-free cookbooks, websites, and apps to find a ton of delicious and inventive meal ideas. Try out different dishes to maintain a varied and fascinating menu.
5. Consider Batch Cooking:
    - Make your meal plan include batch cooking to save time and effort. Make a ton of gluten-free staples, such as grains, proteins, and sauces, so you have plenty to use for several meals a week.
6. Include Snacks:
    - Plan gluten-free snacks to keep you energized between meals. Options like fresh fruit, yogurt, nuts, and gluten-free granola bars are convenient and satisfying choices.
7. Plan for Leftovers:
    - Embrace leftovers as a time-saving strategy. Cook extra portions during dinner to enjoy as lunch the next day, reducing the need for constant meal preparation.
8. Consider Convenience:
    - Acknowledge how handy gluten-free convenience foods like pre-cut veggies, gluten-free meals in a can, and gluten-free pasta are. These can save a lot of time on hectic days.

9. Diversify Protein Sources:
   - Investigate a range of protein sources that are gluten-free, such as quinoa, lean meats, chicken, fish, and legumes. Increasing the variety of proteins you eat guarantees a variety of vital nutrients.
10. Incorporate Gluten-Free Grains:
    - Try including gluten-free grains into your meals, such as amaranth, quinoa, brown rice, and millet, to offer some nutritional diversity. These grains can serve as the foundation for salads, bowls, and side dishes.
11. Plan for Cultural and Ethnic Variety:
    - Infuse variety into your meal plan by exploring gluten-free recipes from different cultures and cuisines. This not only introduces new flavors but also expands your culinary repertoire.
12. Check for Hidden Gluten:
    - Watch out for hidden gluten sources in processed foods, sauces, and condiments. It's important to carefully read labels to make sure the decisions you make fit your gluten-free lifestyle.
13. Plan for Dining Out:
    - When dining out, think about making adjustments or adding meals from gluten-free eateries. Learn about the gluten-free menu items at your neighborhood restaurants so that you can make wise choices.
14. Stay Hydrated:
    - Don't forget about hydration. Include water, herbal teas, and other gluten-free beverages in your meal plan to support overall well-being.
15. Weekly Meal Prep Routine:
    - Establish a weekly meal prep routine that aligns with your schedule. Dedicate time to plan, shop for ingredients, and prepare components of your meals in advance.
16. Adjust Portion Sizes:
    - To make sure you're getting all the nutrients you need without going overboard, pay attention to portion sizes. Based on your exercise level and personal needs, modify the portion amounts.
17. Seek Professional Guidance:
    - Consult with a registered dietitian or nutritionist, especially if you have specific health concerns or dietary restrictions. Professional guidance ensures your meal plan is tailored to your unique needs.
18. Listen to Your Body:
    - Pay attention to how different foods make you feel. Tune into your body's cues and adjust your meal plan accordingly to promote overall well-being.
19. Celebrate Variety:

- Embrace variety in your meal plan to prevent monotony. Incorporate a spectrum of colors, flavors, and textures to make your gluten-free meals both nutritious and enjoyable.

20. Flexibility and Adaptability:

Remain adaptive and flexible. A flexible meal plan enables you to handle unforeseen circumstances without sacrificing your gluten-free lifestyle because life may be unpredictable.

Always keep in mind that the key to designing a successful gluten-free meal plan is to satisfy your nutritional requirements while savoring a wide variety of tasty foods. You may start a delicious, sustainable, and fulfilling gluten-free journey by focusing on whole, naturally gluten-free ingredients, carefully planning ahead, and utilizing a little imagination.

Chapter 4
Morning Bliss: Gluten-Free Breakfast Delights

1. Quinoa Breakfast Bowl

Ingredients:

- one cupful cooked quinoa
- half cupful almond milk
- one tablespoonful honey
- Fresh berries (strawberries, blueberries, raspberries)
- Sliced bananas
- Chopped nuts (almonds, walnuts)

Instructions:

1. Warm the almond milk in a pot and add the quinoa to it.
2. After adding the honey to the quinoa, toss everything together.
3. Spoon into a bowl and garnish with fruit, almonds, and sliced banana.
4. Now go have fun!

Duration: ten minutes

Nutrients: (Per Portion) Caloric content: 350, Amino content: 9g, Fat: 12g, Carb content: 54g, Fiber content: 7g

2. Gluten-Free Banana Pancakes

Ingredients:

- one cupful gluten-free pancake mix
- one ripe banana, mashed
- one cupful almond milk
- one egg
- one tablespoonful coconut oil

Instructions:

1. Smoothly whisk together the pancake mix, egg, banana, and almond milk in a bowl.
2. Grease a griddle with coconut oil and place it over medium heat.
3. For each pancake, use a scant 1/4 cup of batter.
4. When bubbles start to appear on the surface, flip it over and allow the other side to brown.
5. Top with anything you'd like.

Duration: fifteen minutes

Nutrients: (Per Portion) Caloric content: 220, Amino content: 5g, Fat: 8g, Carb content: 32g, Fiber content: 3g

3. Greek Yogurt Parfait

Ingredients:

- one cupful Greek yogurt
- half cupful gluten-free granola
- one-fourth cupful fresh berries
- one tablespoonful honey

Instructions:

1. In a glass or dish, arrange Greek yogurt, gluten-free granola, and several kinds of fresh berries.
2. Simply keep filling it up until it is full.
3. Add a little honey for taste.
4. Continue to make additional servings.

Duration: five minutes

Nutrients: (Per Portion) Caloric content: 280, Amino content: 15g, Fat: 8g, Carb content: 38g, Fiber content: 5g

4. Sweet Potato Hash with Eggs

Ingredients:

- two cupful grated sweet potatoes
- half onion, diced
- one bell pepper, diced
- two tablespoonful olive oil
- Ground black pepper and some salt
- four eggs

Instructions:

1. Heat the olive oil in a pan over medium heat.
2. Add some shredded sweet potatoes, minced onion, and diced bell pepper. Sauté the veggies until they are tender.
3. Split the mixture into four equal parts and put one egg into each part.
4. Once the eggs are covered, cook them to your desired doneness.
5. Add pepper and salt for seasoning.

Duration: twenty minutes

Nutrients: (Per Portion) Caloric content: 280, Amino content: 10g, Fat: 15g, Carb content: 28g, Fiber content: 5g

5. Chia Seed Pudding

Ingredients:

- one-fourth cupful chia seeds
- one cupful almond milk
- one tablespoonful maple syrup
- half teaspoonful vanilla extract
- Fresh fruit for topping

Instructions:

1. Chia seeds, almond milk, maple syrup, and vanilla essence should all be combined in a bowl.
2. Stir occasionally after chilling for at least 4 hours or overnight.
3. Before serving, scatter some fresh fruit on top.

Duration: four hours (chilling time)

Nutrients: (Per Portion) Caloric content: 180, Amino content: 4g, Fat: 10g, Carb content: 20g, Fiber content: 10g

6. Gluten-Free Zucchini Muffins

Ingredients:

- two cupful grated zucchini
- two cupful gluten-free flour
- half cupful coconut oil, melted
- half cupful honey
- two eggs
- one teaspoonful baking powder
- half teaspoonful cinnamon
- one-fourth teaspoonful salt

Instructions:

1. Line a muffin tray with paper liners, then preheat the oven to 350 degrees Fahrenheit (175 degrees Celsius).
2. Grated zucchini, eggs, honey, melted coconut oil, baking powder, cinnamon, and salt should all be added to a bowl. Mix thoroughly until fully incorporated.
3. Spoon the mixture into the muffin cups.
4. When a toothpick put in the center comes out clean, bake for about 25 minutes.

Duration: twenty five minutes

Nutrients: (Per Portion) Caloric content: 180, Amino content: 3g, Fat: 8g, Carb content: 25g, Fiber content: 2g

7. Spinach and Feta Omelette

Ingredients:

- three eggs
- half cupful fresh spinach, chopped
- one-fourth cupful feta cheese, crumbled
- Ground black pepper and some salt
- one tablespoonful olive oil

Instructions:

1. Mix in the salt and pepper after adding the eggs.
2. The olive oil must be heated over medium heat in a skillet.
3. After adding the feta and spinach to the pan, place the eggs inside.
4. When the edges are crispy, fold the omelette in half.
5. Cook for a further two minutes or until the eggs are set through.

Duration: seven minutes

Nutrients: (Per Portion) Caloric content: 280, Amino content: 15g, Fat: 22g, Carb content: 3g, Fiber content: 1g

8. Gluten-Free Breakfast Burrito

Ingredients:

- two gluten-free tortillas
- two eggs, scrambled
- one-fourth cupful black beans, drained and rinsed
- one-fourth cupful diced tomatoes
- one-fourth cupful shredded cheddar cheese
- Salsa for topping

Instructions:

1. The gluten-free tortillas can be heated again in a dry skillet or the microwave.
2. Top some scrambled eggs, diced tomatoes, black beans, and shredded cheddar cheese with a tortilla.
3. Make burritos out of the tortillas and serve them with salsa.

Duration: ten minutes

Nutrients: (Per Portion) Caloric content: 350, Amino content: 15g, Fat: 18g, Carb content: 30g, Fiber content: 6g

9. Gluten-Free Blueberry Muffins

Ingredients:

- one half cupful gluten-free flour
- half cupful almond flour
- half cupful coconut sugar
- one teaspoonful baking powder
- half teaspoonful baking soda
- one-fourth teaspoonful salt
- one cupful blueberries
- half cupful almond milk
- one-fourth cupful coconut oil, melted
- two eggs
- one teaspoonful vanilla extract

Instructions:

1. Line a muffin tray with paper liners, then preheat the oven to 350 degrees Fahrenheit (175 degrees Celsius).
2. Almond flour, coconut sugar, baking powder, baking soda, and salt should all be combined in a basin and put aside.
3. Melted coconut oil, almond milk, blueberries, vanilla extract, and eggs should all be combined in a different bowl. Mix by stirring.
4. Just mix the wet and dry components together.
5. After 18 to 22 minutes of baking, a toothpick inserted in the center of a muffin should come out clean.

Duration: twenty minutes

Nutrients: (Per Portion) Caloric content: 220, Amino content: 4g, Fat: 10g, Carb content: 30g, Fiber content: 3g

10. Gluten-Free Avocado Toast

Ingredients:

- two slices gluten-free bread, toasted
- one ripe avocado
- Cherry tomatoes, sliced
- Red pepper flakes
- Ground black pepper and some salt

Instructions:

1. Spread the mashed avocado on the gluten-free bread.
2. Cherry tomatoes, cut, to serve.
3. For seasoning, add the salt, pepper, and red pepper flakes, if using.

Duration: five minutes

Nutrients: (Per Portion) Caloric content: 280, Amino content: 6g, Fat: 15g, Carb content: 30g, Fiber content: 8g

Chapter 5
Lunchtime Sensations: Flavorful Gluten-Free Creations

11. Quinoa Salad with Lemon Herb Dressing

Ingredients:

- one cupful cooked quinoa
- one cupful cherry tomatoes, halved
- one cucumber, diced
- one-fourth cupful red onion, finely chopped
- one-fourth cupful feta cheese, crumbled
- two tablespoonful fresh parsley, chopped
- three tablespoonful olive oil
- one tablespoonful lemon juice
- Ground black pepper and some salt

Instructions:

1. Quinoa, cherry tomatoes, cucumber, red onion, feta cheese, and parsley should all be combined in a large bowl.
2. In a small bowl, mix together the olive oil, lemon juice, salt, and pepper.
3. Spread the dressing evenly throughout the quinoa mixture.
4. to be served cold.

Duration: twenty minutes

Nutrients: (Per Portion) Caloric content: 280, Amino content: 8g, Fat: 18g, Carb content: 25g, Fiber content: 4g

12. Grilled Chicken and Vegetable Skewers

Ingredients:

- one lb chicken breast, cut into chunks
- one zucchini, sliced
- one red bell pepper, diced
- one red onion, cut into wedges

- two tablespoonful olive oil
- one teaspoonful garlic powder
- one teaspoonful smoked paprika
- Ground black pepper and some salt

Instructions:

1. Preheat the grill or griddle.
2. Combine the chicken, zucchini, red onion, red pepper, smoked paprika, olive oil, and salt & pepper in a bowl.
3. Thread the chicken and veggies onto skewers.
4. Once the vegetables are soft, saute the chicken for 15 to 20 minutes on each side, rotating once.

Duration: twenty minutes

Nutrients: (Per Portion) Caloric content: 320, Amino content: 28g, Fat: 12g, Carb content: 20g, Fiber content: 4g

13. Gluten-Free Caprese Pasta Salad

Ingredients:

- 1 cup gluten-free pasta, cooked
- one cupful cherry tomatoes, halved
- one cupful fresh mozzarella balls
- one-fourth cupful fresh basil, chopped
- three tablespoonful balsamic vinegar
- two tablespoonful olive oil
- Ground black pepper and some salt

Instructions:

1. In a big plate, mix cooked spaghetti, cherry tomatoes, fresh mozzarella, and basil.
2. Mix the olive oil, balsamic vinegar, salt, and pepper in a small basin.
3. Toss the pasta mixture with the dressing after it has been coated evenly.
4. Combine at ambient temperature.

Duration: fifteen minutes

Nutrients: (Per Portion) Caloric content: 340, Amino content: 12g, Fat: 18g, Carb content: 35g, Fiber content: 3g

14. Stuffed Bell Peppers with Quinoa and Black Beans

Ingredients:

- four large bell peppers, halved and seeds removed
- one cupful cooked quinoa
- one can (fifteen oz) black beans, drained and rinsed
- one cupful corn kernels
- one cupful salsa
- one teaspoonful cumin
- half teaspoonful chili powder
- one cupful shredded cheddar cheese

Instructions:

1. Set the cook burner's temperature to 375 degrees.
2. Cooked quinoa, salsa, cumin, chili powder, black beans, and corn should all be combined in a plate.
3. Fill each bell pepper half halfway with a tiny spoonful of the quinoa mixture.
4. Add shredded cheddar cheese on top.
5. Bake peppers for twenty to thirty minutes, or until soft.

Duration: thirty minutes

Nutrients: (Per Portion) Caloric content: 280, Amino content: 15g, Fat: 10g, Carb content: 35g, Fiber content: 8g

15. Gluten-Free Chicken and Vegetable Stir-Fry

Ingredients:

- one lb boneless, skinless chicken breast, sliced
- two cupful broccoli florets
- one bell pepper, thinly sliced
- one carrot, julienned
- two tablespoonful gluten-free soy sauce
- one tablespoonful sesame oil

- one tablespoonful rice vinegar
- one tablespoonful honey
- two tablespoonful olive oil
- two cloves garlic, minced
- one teaspoonful ginger, grated
- Sesame seeds for garnish

Instructions:

1. In a bowl, whisk together the honey, sesame oil, rice vinegar, and soy sauce.
2. In a wok or large pan, heat the olive oil over high heat.
3. After adding, let the chicken brown in the pan.
4. Stir-fry the ginger and garlic for one or two minutes.
5. Add the bell pepper, broccoli, and carrot. Vegetables should be stir-fried until they become crisp-tender.
6. After adding the sauce, toss the chicken and veggies to combine.
7. Serve with rice or quinoa and sprinkle with sesame seeds.

Duration: twenty minutes

Nutrients: (Per Portion) Caloric content: 320, Amino content: 25g, Fat: 12g, Carb content: 25g, Fiber content: 5g

16. Gluten-Free Spinach and Feta Stuffed Chicken Breast

Ingredients:

- four boneless, skinless chicken breasts
- one cupful fresh spinach, chopped
- half cupful feta cheese, crumbled
- two tablespoonful olive oil
- one teaspoonful garlic powder
- one teaspoonful dried oregano
- Ground black pepper and some salt

Instructions:

1. Set the stove burner's temperature to 375°F (190 degrees Celsius).
2. Toss in some chopped spinach, feta cheese, olive oil, garlic powder, dried oregano, salt, and pepper.
3. Create a little bag to provide the bird with a resting place.

4. Put a small amount of spinach and feta into each pocket.
5. Sprinkle salt and pepper on the outside of the chicken breasts.
6. After 25 to 30 minutes in the oven, the chicken should be thoroughly cooked.

Duration: thirty minutes

Nutrients: (Per Portion) Caloric content: 280, Amino content: 30g, Fat: 14g, Carb content: 3g, Fiber content: 1g

17. Gluten-Free Shrimp and Quinoa Bowl

Ingredients:

- one cupful cooked quinoa
- one lb shrimp, peeled and deveined
- two tablespoonful olive oil
- one teaspoonful smoked paprika
- half teaspoonful cumin
- one-fourth teaspoonful cayenne pepper
- Ground black pepper and some salt
- one avocado, sliced
- one-fourth cupful cilantro, chopped
- Lime wedges for portion

Instructions:

1. In a bowl, toss the prawns with the olive oil, cumin, cayenne, smoked paprika, salt, and pepper.
2. The prawns should be cooked in a pan over medium heat until they turn pink and become opaque.
3. Put together bowls with quinoa, prawns, avocado slices, and cilantro.
4. Garnish with wedges of lime.

Duration: fifteen minutes

Nutrients: (Per Portion) Caloric content: 320, Amino content: 25g, Fat: 15g, Carb content: 20g, Fiber content: 5g

18. Gluten-Free Turkey and Vegetable Lettuce Wraps

Ingredients:

- one lb ground turkey
- one tablespoonful olive oil
- one onion, finely chopped
- two cloves garlic, minced
- one teaspoonful ground cumin
- one teaspoonful chili powder
- half teaspoonful smoked paprika
- Ground black pepper and some salt
- Iceberg lettuce leaves
- Salsa and guacamole for portion

Instructions:

1. The olive oil must be heated over medium heat in a skillet.
2. Cook the garlic and onion in the pan until they become translucent.
3. To the ground turkey, add salt, pepper, cumin, chili powder, smoked paprika, and other spices. Browning the turkey will ensure that it is cooked through.
4. Fill lettuce cups with turkey filling and serve.
5. Serve with salsa and guacamole, please.

Duration: twenty minutes

Nutrients: (Per Portion) Caloric content: 280, Amino content: 20g, Fat: 15g, Carb content: 15g, Fiber content: 4g

19. Gluten-Free Eggplant Parmesan

Ingredients:

- one large eggplant, sliced
- one cupful gluten-free breadcrumbs
- one cupful marinara sauce
- one cupful mozzarella cheese, shredded
- one-fourth cupful Parmesan cheese, grated
- Fresh basil for garnish

Instructions:

1. Set the stove burner's temperature to 375°F (190 degrees Celsius).
2. Coat aubergine slices with gluten-free breadcrumbs after dipping them in beaten eggs.
3. Arrange the oiled eggplant slices in a single layer on a baking sheet, and bake for fifteen to twenty minutes.
4. Spread a layer of marinara sauce in a baking dish and top with cooked aubergine pieces and mozzarella cheese.
5. Once more, a final layer of mozzarella is produced.
6. The last step is to add grated Parmesan cheese on top.
7. Bake for a further 20 minutes, or until the cheese melts and is bubbling.
8. Serve with a sprinkling of fresh basil as a garnish.

Duration: Forty minutes

Nutrients: (Per Portion) Caloric content: 280, Amino content: 12g, Fat: 15g, Carb content: 25g, Fiber content: 6g

20. Gluten-Free Teriyaki Salmon Bowl

Ingredients:

- four salmon fillets
- one-fourth cupful gluten-free soy sauce

- two tablespoonful honey
- one tablespoonful rice vinegar
- one teaspoonful sesame oil
- one teaspoonful grated ginger
- two cloves garlic, minced
- four cupful cooked brown rice
- Steamed broccoli florets
- Sliced green onions for garnish

Instructions:

1. Grated ginger, sliced garlic, rice vinegar, honey, and sesame oil should all be combined in a bowl.
2. For half an hour, the salmon fillets should be marinated in the teriyaki sauce.
3. Turn the stove burner up to 400 degrees (200 degrees Celsius).
4. The salmon fillets should be baked for 15 to 20 minutes, depending on how long the marinade took.
5. Serve with steamed broccoli and brown rice.
6. Green onion slices make a lovely garnish.

Duration: thirty minutes

Nutrients: (Per Portion) Caloric content: 380, Amino content: 30g, Fat: 15g, Carb content: 30g, Fiber content: 4g

Chapter 6
Dinner Elegance: Gourmet Gluten-Free Fare

21. Lemon Garlic Herb Roast Chicken

Ingredients:

- one whole chicken (about four lbs)
- four tablespoonful olive oil
- four cloves garlic, minced
- Zest and juice of two lemons
- one tablespoonful fresh rosemary, chopped
- one tablespoonful fresh thyme, chopped
- Ground black pepper and some salt

Instructions:

1. Set the stove burner's temperature to 375°F (190 degrees Celsius).
2. Combine the olive oil, garlic, lemon juice and peel, herbs (thyme and rosemary), salt, and pepper in a bowl.
3. After coating the chicken thoroughly with the herb mixture, move it to a roasting pan.
4. Wait to serve for about 1 hour and 30 minutes, or until the interior temperature reaches 165 degrees Fahrenheit (74 degrees Celsius).
5. Before slicing, it is recommended to let the chicken rest for 10 minutes.

Duration: one hour thirty minutes

Nutrients: (Per Portion) Caloric content: 380, Amino content: 40g, Fat: 22g, Carb content: 2g, Fiber content: 1g

22. Gluten-Free Shrimp Scampi with Zoodles

Ingredients:

- one lb large shrimp, peeled and deveined
- four tablespoonful olive oil
- four cloves garlic, minced
- half teaspoonful red pepper flakes
- Zest and juice of one lemon

- four medium zucchinis, spiralized
- Ground black pepper and some salt
- Fresh parsley for garnish

Instructions:

1. The olive oil must be heated over medium heat in a skillet.
2. Add the garlic and pepper flakes, and cook for one minute.
3. Add a few prawns and the zest and juice of the lemon. The prawns should be cooked until they are pink and opaque.
4. In another pan, sauté the zucchini noodles until they start to get mushy.
5. Serve the zoodles after tossing them in the shrimp sauce.
6. Season with salt and pepper to taste and garnish with fresh parsley.

Duration: fifteen minutes

Nutrients: (Per Portion) Caloric content: 280, Amino content: 25g, Fat: 16g, Carb content: 10g, Fiber content: 3g

23. Gluten-Free Mushroom Risotto

Ingredients:

- one cupful Arborio rice
- half cupful dry white wine
- four cupful gluten-free vegetable broth, heated
- one cupful mushrooms, sliced
- half cupful Parmesan cheese, grated
- two tablespoonful butter
- one small onion, finely chopped
- two cloves garlic, minced
- Ground black pepper and some salt
- Fresh parsley for garnish

Instructions:

1. One tablespoon of butter should be melted over medium heat in a big pan.
2. Cook the garlic and onion in the pan until they become translucent.
3. Let the Arborio rice cook for two minutes.
4. Add the white wine and boil until it has been absorbed.
5. Stirring often, ladle in the heated vegetable broth.

6. Until the rice is creamy and al dente, add extra liquid and stir frequently.
7. Place the cut mushrooms in a different pan and cook them with a tablespoon of butter until they turn golden brown.
8. Toss to combine the Parmesan cheese and mushrooms with the risotto.
9. Season with salt and pepper to taste and garnish with fresh parsley.

Duration: thirty minutes

Nutrients: (Per Portion) Caloric content: 320, Amino content: 8g, Fat: 12g, Carb content: 45g, Fiber content: 2g

24. Gluten-Free Beef Tenderloin with Red Wine Reduction

Ingredients:

- four beef tenderloin steaks
- two tablespoonful olive oil
- Ground black pepper and some salt
- one cupful red wine
- one cupful beef broth
- two tablespoonful balsamic vinegar
- two tablespoonful butter

Instructions:

1. Turn the stove burner up to 400 degrees (200 degrees Celsius).
2. Add salt and pepper to the steaks of beef tenderloin.
3. Heat the olive oil in an ovenproof pan over medium heat.
4. The steaks should be cooked for two to three minutes on each side in a pan that has been heated.
5. Put the pan in the oven and roast for 10 to 12 minutes, depending on how rare you like your meat.
6. Once the steaks have been taken out of the pan, allow them to rest.
7. In the same pan, combine the red wine, beef broth, and balsamic vinegar to create a sauce.
8. Simmer the liquid until it reduces by half.
9. Add the butter and whisk until a creamy sauce is formed.
10. Beef tenderloin steaks are excellent served with a red wine reduction.

Duration: twenty minutes

Nutrients: (Per Portion) Caloric content: 450, Amino content: 35g, Fat: 25g, Carb content: 5g, Fiber content: 0g

25. Gluten-Free Lobster Tail with Garlic Butter

Ingredients:

- four lobster tails
- half cupful unsalted butter, melted
- four cloves garlic, minced
- one tablespoonful fresh parsley, chopped
- Lemon wedges for portion

Instructions:

1. Set the stove burner's temperature to 375°F (190 degrees Celsius).
2. Cut the top of the lobster shell in half vertically using kitchen shears.
3. Remove the lobster meat from the shell gently and with care.
4. The lobster tails should be prepared on a baking sheet.
5. Combine butter, parsley, and garlic in a bowl and whisk to combine.
6. Dredge the lobster tails in the garlic butter mixture.
7. Bake the lobster meat for 15 to 18 minutes, or until it becomes opaque.
8. Present alongside lemon wedges.

Duration: 1eight minutes

Nutrients: (Per Portion) Caloric content: 280, Amino content: 30g, Fat: 18g, Carb content: 1g, Fiber content: 0g

26. Gluten-Free Butternut Squash and Sage Risotto

Ingredients:

- one cupful Arborio rice
- half cupful dry white wine
- four cupful gluten-free vegetable broth, heated
- one cupful butternut squash, diced
- two tablespoonful olive oil
- one small onion, finely chopped
- two cloves garlic, minced

- one tablespoonful fresh sage, chopped
- half cupful Parmesan cheese, grated
- Ground black pepper and some salt

Instructions:

1. Heat the olive oil in a big skillet over medium heat.
2. Cook the garlic and onion in the pan until they become translucent.
3. Let the Arborio rice cook for two minutes.
4. Add the white wine and boil until it has been absorbed.
5. Stirring often, ladle in the heated vegetable broth.
6. Cook the diced butternut squash in olive oil in a separate skillet until it's soft.
7. Add the fresh sage and butternut squash to the risotto and stir.
8. creamy after tossing in Parmesan cheese.
9. Add extra salt and pepper to taste.

Duration: thirty five minutes

Nutrients: (Per Portion) Caloric content: 310, Amino content: 6g, Fat: 10g, Carb content: 45g, Fiber content: 3g

27. Gluten-Free Salmon with Dill Sauce

Ingredients:

- four salmon fillets
- two tablespoonful olive oil
- Ground black pepper and some salt
- one-fourth cupful Greek yogurt
- one tablespoonful Dijon mustard
- one tablespoonful fresh dill, chopped
- one tablespoonful lemon juice

Instructions:

1. Turn the stove burner up to 400 degrees (200 degrees Celsius).
2. Rub salmon fillets with olive oil and season with salt and pepper.
3. The salmon should be boiled for at least 15 minutes, but ideally 20.
4. Combine Greek yoghurt, lemon juice, Dijon mustard, and fresh dill in a bowl.
5. Serve the salmon with the dill sauce..

Duration: twenty minutes

Nutrients: (Per Portion) Caloric content: 320, Amino content: 30g, Fat: 20g, Carb content: 2g, Fiber content: 0g

28. Gluten-Free Beef and Vegetable Stir-Fry

Ingredients:

- one lb flank steak, thinly sliced
- two tablespoonful gluten-free soy sauce
- one tablespoonful rice vinegar
- one tablespoonful honey
- one tablespoonful sesame oil
- two tablespoonful olive oil
- two bell peppers, thinly sliced
- one cupful snow peas
- one carrot, julienned
- two cloves garlic, minced
- one teaspoonful ginger, grated
- Cooked rice for portion

Instructions:

1. Mix the sesame oil, honey, rice vinegar, and soy sauce in a bowl.
2. In a wok or large pan, heat the olive oil over high heat.
3. Add the flank steak and heat it until browned.
4. It's time to take the steak out of the pan and let it rest.
5. Add extra oil as needed and stir-fry veggies (such as bell peppers, snow peas, carrots, garlic, and ginger) in the same skillet until they are crisp-tender.
6. Return the steak to the pan with the sauce once it's done cooking.
7. Toss until all of the ingredients are evenly coated.
8. Accompany with warm rice.

Duration: fifteen minutes

Nutrients: (Per Portion) Caloric content: 380, Amino content: 25g, Fat: 18g, Carb content: 25g, Fiber content: 4g

29. Gluten-Free Chicken Marsala

Ingredients:

- four boneless, skinless chicken breasts
- half cupful gluten-free all-purpose flour
- four tablespoonful olive oil
- eight oz cremini mushrooms, sliced
- one cupful Marsala wine
- one cupful gluten-free chicken broth
- two tablespoonful fresh parsley, chopped
- Ground black pepper and some salt

Instructions:

1. Shake off any excess flour after dredging the chicken breasts.
2. Heat the olive oil in a big skillet over medium heat.
3. Brown the chicken breasts on all sides after adding them to the pan.
4. Once the chicken is out of the pan, place it aside.
5. Brown the mushrooms in the same pan with a little extra oil if you think they'll need it.
6. Pour in the Marsala wine and chicken broth after scraping down the pan.
7. Cook the chicken in the pan until it's cooked through.
8. Add some chopped parsley, salt, and pepper for presentation.

Duration: thirty minutes

Nutrients: (Per Portion) Caloric content: 350, Amino content: 30g, Fat: 14g, Carb content: 20g, Fiber content: 2g

30. Gluten-Free Eggplant and Goat Cheese Stacks

Ingredients:

- one large eggplant, sliced
- one-fourth cupful olive oil
- Ground black pepper and some salt
- four oz goat cheese
- one cupful cherry tomatoes, halved
- Fresh basil for garnish
- Balsamic glaze for drizzling

Instructions:

1. Set the stove burner's temperature to 375°F (190 degrees Celsius).
2. Toss the eggplant slices with olive oil, salt, and pepper.
3. The aubergine slices should be roasted for 15 to 20 minutes, or until they are soft.
4. Cherry tomatoes should be cooked in a pan with a tiny bit of heated olive oil until they are tender.
5. Put sliced eggplant, goat cheese, and butter-cooked cherry tomatoes on top of your stacks.
6. Add the chopped fresh basil and the balsamic glaze.

Duration: twenty minutes

Nutrients: (Per Portion) Caloric content: 280, Amino content: 10g, Fat: 20g, Carb content: 15g, Fiber content: 5g

Chapter 7
Baking Without Limits: Irresistible Gluten-Free Treats

31. Gluten-Free Chocolate Chip Cookies

Ingredients:

- one cupful gluten-free all-purpose flour
- half cupful almond flour
- half cupful unsalted butter, softened
- half cupful brown sugar, packed
- one-fourth cupful granulated sugar
- one large egg
- one teaspoonful vanilla extract
- half teaspoonful baking soda
- one-fourth teaspoonful salt
- one cupful gluten-free chocolate chips

Instructions:

1. Adjust the oven temperature to 350 degrees Fahrenheit and place parchment paper on a baking pan (175 degrees Celsius).
2. In a bowl, mix together butter, brown sugar, and granulated sugar.
3. After adding the egg and vanilla essence, whisk everything together until thoroughly mixed.
4. Add the almond flour, baking soda, and salt to the gluten-free all-purpose flour separately.
5. Stir the dry ingredients into the wet mixture gradually until well incorporated.
6. Add the gluten-free chocolate chips and stir.
7. Spoon dough onto the baking sheet in tablespoon-sized spherical chunks.
8. For ten to twelve minutes, bake them to acquire golden brown edges.
9. Cookies should cool on the baking sheet for five minutes before moving them to a wire rack to finish cooling.

Duration: twelve minutes

Nutrients: (Per Portion) Caloric content: 120, Amino content: 2g, Fat: 8g, Carb content: 12g, Fiber content: 1g

32. Gluten-Free Blueberry Muffins

Ingredients:

- one half cupful gluten-free flour
- half cupful almond flour
- half cupful coconut sugar
- one teaspoonful baking powder
- half teaspoonful baking soda
- one-fourth teaspoonful salt
- one cupful blueberries
- half cupful almond milk
- one-fourth cupful coconut oil, melted
- two eggs
- one teaspoonful vanilla extract

Instructions:

1. Set the oven's temperature to 350 degrees Fahrenheit first (175 degrees Celsius). Next, use paper liners to line a muffin tray.
2. Put all of the dry ingredients in a bowl (almond flour, coconut sugar, gluten-free flour, baking soda, baking powder, and salt).
3. In a separate bowl, beat together almond milk, eggs, melted coconut oil, vanilla extract, and blueberries.
4. Mix the wet and dry components together until they are well combined.
5. When a toothpick inserted in the center comes out clean, bake the muffin cups for 18 to 22 minutes after filling them with batter.
6. Wait until the muffins are completely cool before attempting to take them out of the pan.

Duration: twenty minutes

Nutrients: (Per Portion) Caloric content: 220, Amino content: 4g, Fat: 10g, Carb content: 30g, Fiber content: 3g

33. Gluten-Free Banana Bread

Ingredients:

- three ripe bananas, mashed
- half cupful coconut sugar
- one-fourth cupful unsalted butter, melted
- one-fourth cupful Greek yogurt
- two eggs
- one teaspoonful vanilla extract
- one half cupful gluten-free flour
- one teaspoonful baking soda
- one-fourth teaspoonful salt
- half cupful chopped nuts

Instructions:

1. Grease a loaf pan and preheat the oven to 175 degrees Celsius (about 350 degrees Fahrenheit).
2. In a bowl, combine bananas, eggs, butter, coconut sugar, Greek yoghurt, and vanilla essence.
3. Mix the baking soda, salt, and gluten-free flour in a another basin.
4. Stir the dry ingredients into the wet mixture gradually until well incorporated.
5. Add some chopped nuts if desired.
6. Fill the loaf pan with the batter after it has been heated.
7. When a toothpick inserted in the center comes out clean, bake for 55 to 60 minutes.
8. After the banana bread has cooled for ten minutes, remove it from the pan and let it cool completely on a wire rack.

Duration: 60 minutes

Nutrients: (Per Portion) Caloric content: 180, Amino content: 3g, Fat: 8g, Carb content: 25g, Fiber content: 2g

34. Gluten-Free Lemon Bars

Ingredients:

- one cupful gluten-free all-purpose flour
- half cupful almond flour

- half cupful powdered sugar
- half cupful unsalted butter, softened
- four large eggs
- one half cupful granulated sugar
- one-fourth cupful gluten-free all-purpose flour
- half teaspoonful baking powder
- Zest and juice of two lemons
- Powdered sugar for dusting

Instructions:

1. Preheat the oven to 175°C and prepare a baking dish with parchment paper before proceeding (about 350 degrees Fahrenheit).
2. To form a crumbly mixture, combine melted butter, powdered sugar, almond flour, and gluten-free all-purpose flour in a bowl.
3. To prepare the crust, you can press the ingredients into a baking dish.
4. Make the crust in the oven for fifteen minutes.
5. Whisk the eggs, sugar, baking powder, lemon zest, and lemon juice in a separate basin (all-purpose flour, not gluten-free).
6. The crust should ideally be fried before the lemon mixture is added.
7. To ensure that the edges are crispy, bake for a further twenty-five minutes.
8. Before slicing the lemon bars into squares and sprinkling them with powdered sugar, let them cool completely.

Duration: Forty minutes

Nutrients: (Per Portion) Caloric content: 180, Amino content: 3g, Fat: 8g, Carb content: 25g, Fiber content: 1g

35. Gluten-Free Chocolate Cake

Ingredients:

- one half cupful gluten-free all-purpose flour
- half cupful cocoa powder
- one teaspoonful baking powder
- half teaspoonful baking soda
- one-fourth teaspoonful salt
- one cupful granulated sugar
- half cupful unsalted butter, melted

- two large eggs
- one teaspoonful vanilla extract
- one cupful almond milk

Instructions:

1. Preheat the stove burner to 350 degrees Fahrenheit before buttering a cake pan (175 degrees Celsius).
2. Mix the all-purpose gluten-free flour, baking powder, baking soda, and cocoa powder in a bowl.
3. Combine the butter, eggs, vanilla, and powdered sugar in a another bowl.
4. Gradually stir in the dry ingredients and almond milk in turns until the liquid mixture is well combined.
5. Transfer the cake mixture into the prepared pan.
6. When a toothpick inserted in the center comes out clean, bake for 25 to 30 minutes.
7. Give the chocolate cake time to cool before frosting or serving.

Duration: thirty minutes

Nutrients: (Per Portion) Caloric content: 200, Amino content: 3g, Fat: 10g, Carb content: 25g, Fiber content: 2g

36. Gluten-Free Apple Crisp

Ingredients:

- four cupful sliced apples
- two tablespoonful lemon juice
- half cupful gluten-free all-purpose flour
- half cupful rolled oats
- half cupful brown sugar
- one-fourth cupful almond flour
- one-fourth cupful melted butter
- one teaspoonful cinnamon
- one-fourth teaspoonful nutmeg
- Vanilla ice cream for portion

Instructions:

1. Before anything else, grease a baking dish and heat the oven to 175°C (about 350 degrees Fahrenheit).
2. Coat a baking dish with nonstick cooking spray to get it ready.
3. To make the dry ingredients, combine the rolled oats, brown sugar, almond flour, melted butter, cinnamon, and nutmeg in a separate bowl. Next, confirm that the flour is free of gluten.
4. Ensure that the apples have an even layer of topping on them.
5. Bake for 35 to 40 minutes, until the topping is golden brown and the apples are soft.
6. Before serving, let the apple crisp cool to the touch.
7. Add a dollop of vanilla ice cream on top if you'd like.

Duration: Forty minutes

Nutrients: (Per Portion) Caloric content: 220, Amino content: 2g, Fat: 10g, Carb content: 30g, Fiber content: 4g

37. Gluten-Free Pumpkin Bread

Ingredients:

- one 3/four cupful gluten-free all-purpose flour
- one teaspoonful baking soda
- half teaspoonful baking powder
- half teaspoonful salt
- one teaspoonful ground cinnamon
- half teaspoonful ground nutmeg
- one-fourth teaspoonful ground cloves
- half cupful unsalted butter, melted
- one cupful canned pumpkin puree
- one cupful granulated sugar
- half cupful brown sugar, packed
- two large eggs
- one teaspoonful vanilla extract
- one-fourth cupful water

Instructions:

1. Grease a loaf pan and preheat the oven to 175 degrees Celsius (about 350 degrees Fahrenheit).
2. All-purpose gluten-free flour, baking powder, baking soda, salt, nutmeg, cinnamon, and cloves should all be combined in a bowl.
3. Melt the butter and combine it with the eggs, water, vanilla, brown and white sugars, and pumpkin puree in a different bowl.
4. Stir the dry ingredients into the wet mixture gradually until well incorporated.
5. Fill the loaf pan with the batter after it has been heated.
6. A toothpick inserted in the center should come out clean after baking for 60 to 65 minutes.
7. Slice the pumpkin bread once it has had time to cool.

Duration: 6five minutes

Nutrients: (Per Portion) Caloric content: 180, Amino content: 2g, Fat: 8g, Carb content: 25g, Fiber content: 2g

38. Gluten-Free Raspberry Almond Bars

Ingredients:

- one half cupful gluten-free all-purpose flour
- half cupful almond flour
- half cupful granulated sugar
- half teaspoonful almond extract
- one cupful unsalted butter, softened
- half cupful raspberry jam
- half cupful sliced almonds

Instructions:

1. Preheat the oven to 175°C and prepare a baking dish with parchment paper before proceeding (about 350 degrees Fahrenheit).
2. Combine all-purpose gluten-free flour, almond flour, sugar, melted butter, and almond essence in a bowl and stir until crumbly.
3. Using one cup of the mixture for the topping, press the remaining mixture into the bottom of the prepared baking dish.
4. Bake for 12 to 15 minutes, or until a little browning occurs on the crust.
5. When the crust is done, cover it with raspberry jam.
6. Cover the jam with a layer of the prepared crumb mixture and some sliced almonds.
7. Bake for an additional 25 minutes, or until the top is completely browned.

8. Before slicing the raspberry almond bars into squares, make sure they have cooled fully.

Duration: Forty minutes

Nutrients: (Per Portion) Caloric content: 200, Amino content: 2g, Fat: 12g, Carb content: 20g, Fiber content: 1g

39. Gluten-Free Chocolate Avocado Mousse

Ingredients:

- two ripe avocados, peeled and pitted
- half cupful cocoa powder
- half cupful coconut milk
- half cupful maple syrup
- one teaspoonful vanilla extract
- Pinch of salt
- Fresh berries for garnish

Instructions:

1. Ripe avocados, chocolate powder, coconut milk, maple syrup, vanilla extract, and a dash of salt should all be combined in a food processor or blender.
2. Mix until thoroughly mixed and smooth.
3. The chocolate avocado mousse needs to be refrigerated for at least two hours to rest.
4. Serve cold, garnished with fresh berries.

Duration: ten minutes (plus chilling time)

Nutrients: (Per Portion) Caloric content: 180, Amino content: 3g, Fat: 14g, Carb content: 20g, Fiber content: 6g

40. Gluten-Free Cookies

Ingredients:

- one cupful gluten-free all-purpose flour
- half teaspoonful baking soda
- one-fourth teaspoonful salt
- half cupful unsalted butter, softened
- half cupful brown sugar, packed
- one-fourth cupful granulated sugar
- one large egg
- one teaspoonful vanilla extract
- one cupful gluten-free chocolate chips

Instructions:

1. Adjust the oven temperature to 350 degrees Fahrenheit and place parchment paper on a baking pan (175 degrees Celsius).
2. Mix the flour, baking powder, and salt in a bowl.
3. Beat butter, brown sugar, and white sugar in a another basin until foamy.
4. Add the egg and the extract of vanilla and beat.
5. Stir the dry ingredients into the wet mixture gradually until well incorporated.
6. Add the gluten-free chocolate chips and stir.
7. Spoon dough onto the baking sheet in tablespoon-sized spherical chunks.
8. Bake for an additional minute or two if you want golden edges.
9. Let the cookies cool on the baking sheet for five minutes before moving them to a wire rack.

Duration: twelve minutes

Nutrients: (Per Portion) Caloric content: 180, Amino content: 2g, Fat: 10g, Carb content: 22g, Fiber content: 1g

Chapter 8
International Flavors, Gluten-Free Style

41. Thai Basil Chicken (Pad Krapow Gai)

Ingredients:

- one lb boneless, skinless chicken breast, minced
- two tablespoonful gluten-free soy sauce
- one tablespoonful fish sauce
- one tablespoonful oyster sauce
- one tablespoonful sugar
- four cloves garlic, minced
- one shallot, thinly sliced
- one cupful fresh basil leaves
- two tablespoonful vegetable oil
- Red pepper flakes for garnish
- Cooked rice for portion

Instructions:

1. In a bowl, mix together the soy sauce, oyster sauce, fish sauce, and sugar.
2. In a wok or large pan, heat the vegetable oil over high heat.
3. Brown the chicken mince while it's cooking.
4. Stir-fry the garlic and shallot for one to two minutes.
5. Mix the chicken thoroughly after adding the sauce.
6. Add some fresh basil leaves and let them wilt in the heat.
7. Add some crushed red pepper flakes on top for flavor.
8. Serve warm rice alongside.

Duration: fifteen minutes

Nutrients: (Per Portion) Caloric content: 320, Amino content: 25g, Fat: 15g, Carb content: 15g, Fiber content: 2g

42. Mango and Avocado Salsa with Shrimp Tacos

Ingredients:

- one lb shrimp, peeled and deveined
- one tablespoonful olive oil
- one teaspoonful chili powder
- Ground black pepper and some salt
- two ripe mangoes, diced
- one avocado, diced
- one-fourth cupful red onion, finely chopped
- one-fourth cupful fresh cilantro, chopped
- Juice of two limes
- Corn tortillas for portion

Instructions:

1. Coat the prawns in olive oil, chilli powder, salt, and pepper in a bowl.
2. Shrimp should be fried in a skillet over medium heat until they are pink and opaque.
3. In a separate meal, combine diced mangoes with avocado, red onion, cilantro, lime juice, and salt.
4. Potato tortillas, somewhat warm.
5. Place the prawns inside the taco shells, then add smashed mango and avocado salsa on top.

Duration: ten minutes

Nutrients: (Per Portion) Caloric content: 280, Amino content: 20g, Fat: 15g, Carb content: 25g, Fiber content: 5g

43. Indian Butter Chicken (Murgh Makhani)

Ingredients:

- one lb boneless, skinless chicken thighs, cut into chunks
- one cupful plain yogurt
- two tablespoonful gluten-free garam masala
- one tablespoonful ground turmeric
- one tablespoonful ground cumin
- one tablespoonful ground coriander
- one teaspoonful chili powder

- one teaspoonful paprika
- four cloves garlic, minced
- one tablespoonful fresh ginger, grated
- half cupful tomato puree
- half cupful heavy cream
- one-fourth cupful unsalted butter
- Fresh cilantro for garnish
- Cooked rice for portion

Instructions:

1. In a bowl, mix yogurt, paprika, coriander, ginger, garlic, turmeric, cumin, and chili powder.
2. Let the chicken marinate in the fridge for at least an hour.
3. In a skillet over medium heat, melt the butter.
4. When the chicken is added, let it simmer until browned.
5. Stir in the entire milk and canned tomatoes.
6. Simmer the chicken for a further 15 to 20 minutes, or until it's cooked through.
7. Add fresh cilantro as a garnish.
8. Serve warm rice alongside.

Duration: thirty minutes

Nutrients: (Per Portion) Caloric content: 380, Amino content: 25g, Fat: 25g, Carb content: 15g, Fiber content: 2g

44. Greek Quinoa Salad with Lemon Herb Dressing

Ingredients:

- one cupful quinoa, cooked
- one cucumber, diced
- one cupful cherry tomatoes, halved
- half cupful Kalamata olives, pitted and sliced
- half cupful feta cheese, crumbled
- one-fourth cupful red onion, finely chopped
- two tablespoonful olive oil
- Juice of one lemon
- one teaspoonful dried oregano
- Ground black pepper and some salt

Instructions:

1. In a large bowl, mix together the red onion, cucumber, cherry tomatoes, feta cheese, and olives.
2. In a small bowl, add olive oil, lemon juice, oregano, salt, and pepper.
3. After pouring the dressing over the quinoa mixture, toss to fully combine.
4. Use ice for serving.

Duration: fifteen minutes

Nutrients: (Per Portion) Caloric content: 280, Amino content: 8g, Fat: 18g, Carb content: 25g, Fiber content: 4g

45. Japanese-inspired Miso Glazed Salmon

Ingredients:

- four salmon fillets
- one-fourth cupful gluten-free miso paste
- two tablespoonful honey
- two tablespoonful gluten-free soy sauce
- one tablespoonful rice vinegar
- one teaspoonful sesame oil
- two teaspoonful fresh ginger, grated
- two cloves garlic, minced
- Green onions for garnish
- Sesame seeds for garnish
- Cooked white or brown rice for portion

Instructions:

1. Elevate the burner on the stove to 400 degrees (200 degrees Celsius).
2. Combine the miso paste, ginger, garlic, sesame oil, rice vinegar, honey, and soy sauce in a bowl.
3. Place the salmon fillets on a baking sheet lined with parchment paper so that they are in a single layer.
4. Apply the miso glaze to the salmon.
5. Sear the salmon for 12 to 15 minutes, flipping once, or until it's opaque throughout.
6. Place the sliced green onions on top, followed by a scattering of toasted sesame seeds.
7. Serve warm rice alongside.

Duration: fifteen minutes

Nutrients: (Per Portion) Caloric content: 320, Amino content: 30g, Fat: 15g, Carb content: 20g, Fiber content: 2g

46. Mexican Quinoa Stuffed Peppers

Ingredients:

- four bell peppers, halved and seeds removed
- one cupful quinoa, cooked
- one can black beans, drained and rinsed
- one cupful corn kernels (fresh or frozen)
- one cupful salsa
- one teaspoonful ground cumin
- one teaspoonful chili powder
- Ground black pepper and some salt
- one cupful shredded cheddar cheese
- Fresh cilantro for garnish

Instructions:

1. Adjust the temperature of the stove burner to 375°F (190 degrees Celsius).
2. In a large bowl, combine cooked quinoa, black beans, corn, salsa, cumin, chili powder, salt, and pepper.
3. Spoon mixture of quinoa into half of bell peppers.
4. Every filled pepper needs to have some shredded cheddar cheese on top of it.
5. Bake peppers for 20 to 30 minutes, or until they become tender.
6. Add fresh cilantro as a garnish.
7. Serve extra salsa on the side if you'd like it.

Duration: thirty minutes

Nutrients: (Per Portion) Caloric content: 280, Amino content: 10g, Fat: 12g, Carb content: 35g, Fiber content: 6g

47. Italian-inspired Caprese Chicken

Ingredients:

- four boneless, skinless chicken breasts
- two tablespoonful olive oil
- one teaspoonful Italian seasoning
- Ground black pepper and some salt
- one cupful cherry tomatoes, halved
- one cupful fresh mozzarella, sliced
- Balsamic glaze for drizzling
- Fresh basil leaves for garnish
- Cooked quinoa or pasta for portion

Instructions:

1. Adjust the temperature of the stove burner to 375°F (190 degrees Celsius).
2. Season chicken breasts with salt, pepper, and Italian seasoning. Drizzle it with some olive oil.
3. In a skillet that is oven-safe, sear the chicken on all sides.
4. Every single chicken breast looks fantastic with the cherry tomatoes sliced in half and the fresh mozzarella slices on top.
5. Bake the dish for 25 minutes to make sure the cheese is melted and bubbling and the chicken is cooked through.
6. The last touches are fresh basil and a balsamic glaze.
7. Garnish with cooked quinoa or spaghetti and serve.

Duration: twenty five minutes

Nutrients: (Per Portion) Caloric content: 320, Amino content: 30g, Fat: 18g, Carb content: 10g, Fiber content: 2g

48. Moroccan-inspired Quinoa Tagine

Ingredients:

- one cupful quinoa, cooked
- one tablespoonful olive oil
- one onion, finely chopped
- two cloves garlic, minced

- one teaspoonful ground cumin
- one teaspoonful ground coriander
- one teaspoonful ground cinnamon
- half teaspoonful ground turmeric
- half teaspoonful paprika
- half teaspoonful cayenne pepper
- one can chickpeas, drained and rinsed
- one cupful diced tomatoes
- one cupful vegetable broth
- one cupful diced carrots
- one cupful chopped dried apricots
- Ground black pepper and some salt
- Fresh cilantro for garnish

Instructions:

1. In a large pan, the olive oil should be heated over medium heat.
2. Sauté the onion and garlic until they are soft.
3. Add the cayenne pepper, cinnamon, turmeric, paprika, ground cumin, and coriander. For about two minutes, heat.
4. Stir the cooked quinoa, chickpeas, diced tomatoes, and vegetable broth with the carrots and dried apricots.
5. To taste, add more salt and pepper.
6. Carrots should be fork-tender after 15 to 20 minutes of simmering while covered.
7. Add fresh cilantro as a garnish.
8. Use as the meal's principal course.

Duration: twenty minutes

Nutrients: (Per Portion) Caloric content: 300, Amino content: 10g, Fat: 8g, Carb content: 50g, Fiber content: 8g

49. Brazilian-inspired Chicken Coxinha

Ingredients:

- two cupful shredded cooked chicken
- one cupful tapioca flour
- one cupful chicken broth
- half cupful milk
- two tablespoonful butter
- one teaspoonful salt
- half teaspoonful ground black pepper
- half cupful cream cheese
- two cupful gluten-free breadcrumbs
- Vegetable oil for frying

Instructions:

1. In a pot, add the tapioca flour, chicken broth, milk, butter, salt, and pepper; stir to a smooth consistency.
2. Stirring often, cook over medium heat until mixture thickens and forms dough.
3. Once the heat is off, give it a minute or two to cool.
4. Cream cheese and shredded chicken should be added to the dough mixture.
5. Shape the mixture into croquettes or little balls.
6. Roll each ball into an even layer of gluten-free breadcrumbs.
7. Turn the heat up to 350 degrees Fahrenheit and grease a big pan or deep fryer with vegetable oil (180 degrees Celsius).
8. Cook the chicken coxinha in oil until it becomes crispy and brown.
9. squander water on paper towels.
10. This tasty Brazilian snack is best served warm..

Duration: twenty minutes

Nutrients: (Per Portion) Caloric content: 220, Amino content: 15g, Fat: 10g, Carb content: 18g, Fiber content: 1g

50. Spanish-inspired Paella with Chorizo and Seafood

Ingredients:

- two cupful gluten-free paella rice
- half lb chorizo sausage, sliced
- one lb mixed seafood (shrimp, mussels, clams)
- one onion, finely chopped
- two bell peppers, sliced
- four cloves garlic, minced
- one teaspoonful smoked paprika
- one teaspoonful saffron threads
- half cupful white wine
- four cupful gluten-free chicken broth
- one cupful frozen peas
- Lemon wedges for portion
- Fresh parsley for garnish

Instructions:

1. In a small basin, soak the saffron threads in white wine.
2. In a large skillet or paella pan, brown the chorizo slices.
3. Add some finely chopped peppers, onions, and garlic. Heat gently until vegetables are soft.
4. Add some saffron-flavored wine, smoked paprika, and paella rice.
5. After adding the chicken broth, turn down the heat.
6. Make sure the fish is completely submerged by placing it over the rice and liquid.
7. Cook the rice and fish until they are tender.
8. After adding frozen peas, cover and boil until the peas are tender.

9. Garnish with fresh parsley and serve with lemon wedges.

Duration: Forty minutes

Nutrients: (Per Portion) Caloric content: 380, Amino content: 20g, Fat: 15g, Carb content: 45g, Fiber content: 3g

Chapter 9
Hearty and Wholesome: Gluten-Free Comfort Foods

51. Gluten-Free Chicken and Rice Casserole

Ingredients:

- two cupful cooked and shredded chicken
- two cupful cooked white rice
- one cupful gluten-free chicken broth
- one cupful gluten-free cream of mushroom soup
- one cupful frozen peas and carrots
- half cupful diced onion
- two cloves garlic, minced
- one teaspoonful dried thyme
- Ground black pepper and some salt
- one cupful shredded cheddar cheese

Instructions:

1. The burner should first be heated to 175 degrees Celsius (around 350 degrees Fahrenheit).
2. In a large bowl, mix together cooked rice, shredded chicken, cream of mushroom soup, frozen peas and carrots, minced garlic, chopped onion, dried thyme, salt, and pepper.
3. Transfer the contents of the bowl to a casserole dish that has been buttered.
4. Top with shredded cheddar cheese.
5. Bake the casserole for 25 to 30 minutes, or until it is hot and bubbling and the cheese is melted and browned.
6. Before slicing, let it cool for a few minutes.

Duration: thirty minutes

Nutrients: (Per Portion) Caloric content: 320, Amino content: 20g, Fat: 15g, Carb content: 25g, Fiber content: 3g

52. Gluten-Free Beef Stew

Ingredients:

- one and a half lbs stew beef, cubed
- three cupful gluten-free beef broth
- two carrots, peeled and sliced
- two potatoes, peeled and diced
- one cupful chopped celery
- one onion, diced
- two cloves garlic, minced
- two tablespoonful gluten-free tomato paste
- one teaspoonful dried thyme
- one teaspoonful dried rosemary
- Ground black pepper and some salt
- two tablespoonful olive oil

Instructions:

1. Heat the olive oil in a big saucepan over medium heat.
2. Brown the beef cubes on each sides after adding them.
3. Once the onions and garlic have softened from their sautéing, add them.
4. Add the tomato paste, salt, pepper, thyme, and rosemary and stir.
5. Add the beef broth and heat until it begins to boil.
6. After the steak is cooked, simmer it for one and a half to two hours while covered with reduced heat.
7. Add some chopped celery, sliced carrots, and diced potatoes.
8. Cook the vegetables for a further half hour, or until they are thoroughly cooked.
9. Adjust the seasoning as necessary right before serving.

Duration: two and a half hours

Nutrients: (Per Portion) Caloric content: 380, Amino content: 25g, Fat: 15g, Carb content: 30g, Fiber content: 4g

53. Gluten-Free Spinach and Feta Stuffed Chicken Breasts

Ingredients:

- four boneless, skinless chicken breasts

- two cupful fresh spinach, chopped
- half cupful crumbled feta cheese
- two tablespoonful olive oil
- one teaspoonful dried oregano
- one teaspoonful garlic powder
- Ground black pepper and some salt
- Toothpicks

Instructions:

1. First, adjust the temperature of the burner to 190 degrees Celsius (about 375 degrees Fahrenheit).
2. The olive oil must be heated over medium heat in a skillet.
3. Toss in some chopped spinach and let it wilt in the pan.
4. Combine the feta cheese, wilted spinach, dried oregano, garlic powder, salt, and pepper in a bowl.
5. Cut a horizontal slice down the center of each chicken breast to form a pocket.
6. Take each chicken breast and stuff it with the spinach and feta mixture.
7. Use toothpicks to seal the pockets.
8. Sprinkle salt and pepper on the outside of the chicken breasts.
9. Pack the chicken breasts and arrange them in a baking dish.
10. After 25 to 30 minutes in the oven, the chicken should be thoroughly cooked.

Duration: thirty minutes

Nutrients: (Per Portion) Caloric content: 320, Amino content: 30g, Fat: 15g, Carb content: 5g, Fiber content: 2g

54. Gluten-Free Turkey and Vegetable Meatloaf

Ingredients:

- one and a half lbs ground turkey
- one cupful gluten-free breadcrumbs
- half cupful grated zucchini, squeezed to remove excess moisture
- half cupful grated carrot
- half cupful chopped onion
- two cloves garlic, minced
- one-fourth cupful gluten-free ketchup
- two tablespoonful Worcestershire sauce (make sure it's gluten-free)

- one teaspoonful dried thyme
- one teaspoonful dried rosemary
- Ground black pepper and some salt
- one egg, beaten

Instructions:

1. First, adjust the temperature of the burner to 190 degrees Celsius (about 375 degrees Fahrenheit).
2. Ground turkey, gluten-free breadcrumbs, sautéed onions, garlic, zucchini, carrots, ketchup, Worcestershire sauce, dried thyme, dried rosemary, salt, and pepper should all be combined in a substantial bowl.
3. Continue mixing when all of the ingredients have been evenly distributed.
4. Shape the ingredients into a loaf and put it in an oiled baking dish.
5. Bake for 45 to 50 minutes, or until an instant-read thermometer registers 165F/74C.
6. Before slicing, let the meatloaf stand for 10 minutes.

Duration: 50 minutes

Nutrients: (Per Portion) Caloric content: 280, Amino content: 25g, Fat: 12g, Carb content: 15g, Fiber content: 3g

55. Gluten-Free Chicken and Broccoli Alfredo Bake

Ingredients:

- two cupful cooked and shredded chicken
- two cupful broccoli florets, blanched
- two cupful gluten-free pasta, cooked al dente
- two cupful gluten-free Alfredo sauce
- one cupful shredded mozzarella cheese
- half cupful grated Parmesan cheese
- two cloves garlic, minced
- one teaspoonful dried Italian herbs
- Ground black pepper and some salt

Instructions:

1. First, adjust the temperature of the burner to 190 degrees Celsius (about 375 degrees Fahrenheit).

2. The chicken shreds, blanched broccoli, gluten-free pasta, Alfredo sauce, garlic, dried Italian herbs, salt, and pepper should all be combined in a big platter.
3. Pour the mixture into a baking dish that has been oiled.
4. Add grated Parmesan cheese and shredded mozzarella on top.
5. Bake until the cheese is melted and bubbling, about 25 minutes.
6. Allow the bake to cool for a few minutes before serving.

Duration: twenty five minutes

Nutrients: (Per Portion) Caloric content: 380, Amino content: 30g, Fat: 18g, Carb content: 25g, Fiber content: 3g

56. Gluten-Free Sweet Potato and Black Bean Chili

Ingredients:

- two sweet potatoes, peeled and diced
- one can black beans, drained and rinsed
- one can diced tomatoes
- one onion, diced
- two cloves garlic, minced
- one bell pepper, diced
- two cupful gluten-free vegetable broth
- one tablespoonful chili powder
- one teaspoonful ground cumin
- one teaspoonful smoked paprika
- Ground black pepper and some salt
- Fresh cilantro for garnish
- Sour cream for portion

Instructions:

1. Sweet potatoes, black beans, chopped onions, diced tomatoes, minced garlic, diced bell pepper, vegetable broth, cumin, smoked paprika, chilli powder, salt, and pepper should all be combined in a big saucepan. Mix everything together.
2. After bringing the chili to a boil, turn down the heat to a low simmer.
3. Cover and simmer the sweet potatoes for 30 to 40 minutes, or until they are fork-tender.
4. As necessary, adjust the seasoning.
5. Serve the hot, spicy chilli with sour cream and fresh cilantro on top.

Duration: Forty minutes

Nutrients: (Per Portion) Caloric content: 250, Amino content: 8g, Fat: 1g, Carb content: 55g, Fiber content: 10g

57. Gluten-Free Shepherd's Pie

Ingredients:

- one and a half lbs ground lamb or beef
- one onion, diced
- two carrots, peeled and diced
- one cupful frozen peas
- two cloves garlic, minced
- one cupful gluten-free beef broth
- two tablespoonful gluten-free tomato paste
- one teaspoonful dried thyme
- Ground black pepper and some salt
- four cupful mashed sweet potatoes

Instructions:

1. Achieving a temperature of 190 degrees Celsius on the burner is the first step (about 375 degrees Fahrenheit).
2. A skillet over medium heat is ideal for cooking ground lamb or beef.
3. Toss in some minced garlic, frozen peas, carrots, and onions. Gently cook the veggies until they're tender.
4. Add the tomato paste, dried thyme, salt, pepper, beef broth, and mix well.
5. For another 10–15 minutes, or until the sauce thickens, keep simmering gently.
6. Grease a baking dish and add the meat and vegetable mixture.
7. On top, you should spread mashed sweet potatoes.
8. Bake for 25-30 minutes to get a golden brown top.
9. The shepherd's pie needs a few minutes to cool before it can be served.

Duration: thirty minutes

Nutrients: (Per Portion) Caloric content: 380, Amino content: 20g, Fat: 15g, Carb content: 40g, Fiber content: 7g

58. Gluten-Free Quinoa and Vegetable Stir-Fry

Ingredients:

- one cupful quinoa, cooked
- two cupful mixed vegetables (broccoli, bell peppers, snap peas, carrots)
- one cupful gluten-free teriyaki sauce
- two tablespoonful sesame oil
- two cloves garlic, minced
- one teaspoonful fresh ginger, grated
- one tablespoonful gluten-free soy sauce
- one tablespoonful rice vinegar
- Sesame seeds for garnish
- Green onions for garnish

Instructions:

1. Put the sesame oil into a big pan or wok and heat it over medium heat.
2. Add the minced garlic and grated ginger and stir-fry for one minute.
3. Throw in a bunch of veggies and sauté them until they're tender and crunchy.
4. It is time to add the cooked quinoa.
5. Whisk together the teriyaki sauce, rice vinegar, and gluten-free soy sauce in a small bowl.
6. Once the sauce has been added, combine it with the quinoa and vegetables.
7. Just a couple more minutes in the pan will bring it up to temperature.
8. Shred some green onions and sprinkle some sesame seeds on top.

Duration: fifteen minutes

Nutrients: (Per Portion) Caloric content: 320, Amino content: 10g, Fat: 12g, Carb content: 45g, Fiber content: 7g

59. Gluten-Free Eggplant Parmesan

Ingredients:

- two large eggplants, sliced
- two cupful gluten-free marinara sauce
- two cupful shredded mozzarella cheese
- half cupful grated Parmesan cheese
- one cupful gluten-free breadcrumbs

- two teaspoonful dried Italian herbs
- Ground black pepper and some salt
- Fresh basil for garnish

Instructions:

1. Achieving a temperature of 190 degrees Celsius on the burner is the first step (about 375 degrees Fahrenheit).
2. Set the sliced eggplants aside for 30 minutes after salting to soak up any excess moisture.
3. The eggplant should be washed, sliced, and dried with paper towels.
4. Whisk together the gluten-free breadcrumbs and dried Italian herbs in a small bowl.
5. Pour the breadcrumb mixture over the eggplant slices.
6. Spread the marinara sauce, mozzarella, Parmesan, and cut eggplants in an oiled baking dish.
7. Once all the ingredients have been used, continue layering and top with cheese.
8. Allow the cheese to melt and bubble for around 30 to 35 minutes in the oven.
9. Before serving, garnish with a handful of fresh basil.

Duration: thirty five minutes

Nutrients: (Per Portion) Caloric content: 280, Amino content: 15g, Fat: 15g, Carb content: 25g, Fiber content: 5g

60. Gluten-Free Chicken Pot Pie

Ingredients:

- two cupful cooked and shredded chicken
- one cupful frozen mixed vegetables (peas, carrots, corn)
- half cupful gluten-free chicken broth
- half cupful gluten-free cream of chicken soup
- two tablespoonful unsalted butter
- two tablespoonful gluten-free all-purpose flour
- one teaspoonful dried thyme
- Ground black pepper and some salt
- one gluten-free pie crust (store-bought or homemade)

Instructions:

1. Prior to cooking meals at 425 degrees Fahrenheit, the burner must be heated (220 degrees Celsius).
2. Put the butter in a saucepan and melt it over medium heat.
3. Add the thyme, salt, pepper, and all-purpose gluten-free flour; mix until combined.
4. Add the chicken broth and cream of chicken soup in small increments while stirring continuously until the desired consistency is achieved.
5. Throw the frozen veggies and shredded chicken into a big bowl and mix well.
6. Toss the chicken, veggies, and thickened sauce together.
7. Make sure to oil your pie pan before rolling out the gluten-free dough.
8. Put the chicken and veggie mixture into the pie crust.

9. Seal the edges by covering them with a second pie shell.
10. Let the steam out by slicing the top crust.
11. After 30–35 minutes in the oven, the crust should be golden brown.
12. It's best to wait a few minutes for the chicken pot pie to cool before slicing.

Duration: thirty five minutes

Nutrients: (Per Portion) Caloric content: 350, Amino content: 20g, Fat: 18g, Carb content: 30g, Fiber content: 4g

Chapter 10
Sweet Endings: Delectable Gluten-Free Desserts

61. Gluten-Free Chocolate Chip Cookies

Ingredients:

- two cupful gluten-free all-purpose flour
- one teaspoonful baking soda
- half teaspoonful salt
- one cupful unsalted butter, softened
- one cupful brown sugar, packed
- half cupful granulated sugar
- two large eggs
- two teaspoonful vanilla extract
- two cupful gluten-free chocolate chips

Instructions:

1. It is necessary to bring the burner up to 175 degrees Celsius before using it (around 350 degrees Fahrenheit).
2. Flour that is free of gluten, baking soda, and salt should be mixed together in a basin.
3. To make the sugar foam, put the brown sugar, white sugar, and softened butter in a large bowl and mix until combined.
4. Add the eggs one by one and beat until well blended. Blend in the vanilla flavoring.
5. Add the dry ingredients to the wet ones gradually, blending after each addition.
6. Combine with gluten-free chocolate chips and mix well.
7. Pinch the dough and put spoonfuls onto a parchment-lined baking sheet.
8. Ten to twelve minutes in the oven will give them a golden brown crust.
9. Let the cookies cool for five minutes on the baking sheet before moving them to a wire rack.

Duration: twelve minutes

Nutrients: (Per Portion) Caloric content: 180, Amino content: 2g, Fat: 10g, Carb content: 24g, Fiber content: 1g

62. Gluten-Free Flourless Chocolate Cake

Ingredients:

- one cupful unsalted butter
- one cupful dark chocolate, chopped
- one cupful granulated sugar
- half cupful cocoa powder
- one-fourth teaspoonful salt
- four large eggs
- one teaspoonful vanilla extract
- Powdered sugar for dusting

Instructions:

1. Achieving a temperature of 190 degrees Celsius on the burner is the first step (about 375 degrees Fahrenheit). Pat down and grease a 9-inch cake pan.
2. Put the butter and dark chocolate in a bowl that can withstand heat and melt them together. To achieve a smooth consistency, stir for a short while.
3. Incorporate the cocoa powder, sugar, and salt into the chocolate mixture while stirring.
4. After pounding in the eggs one by one, add the vanilla essence.
5. Once the pan is hot, pour in the cake batter.
6. When a toothpick inserted in the middle comes out with moist crumbs, bake for 25 to 30 minutes.
7. Before moving the cake to a serving dish, let it cool in the pan for about 10 minutes.
8. Powdered sugar should be sprinkled on top of each dish.

Duration: thirty minutes

Nutrients: (Per Portion) Caloric content: 280, Amino content: 4g, Fat: 20g, Carb content: 25g, Fiber content: 2g

63. Gluten-Free Lemon Bars

Ingredients:

- one cupful gluten-free all-purpose flour
- half cupful powdered sugar
- half cupful unsalted butter, softened
- two large eggs

- one cupful granulated sugar
- two tablespoonful gluten-free all-purpose flour
- half teaspoonful baking powder
- one-fourth teaspoonful salt
- Zest and juice of two lemons
- Powdered sugar for dusting

Instructions:

1. It is necessary to bring the burner up to 175 degrees Celsius before using it (around 350 degrees Fahrenheit). Pat down a baking dish that measures 9 by 9 inches.
2. Combine the melted butter, powdered sugar, and gluten-free flour in a big basin and beat until combined. Spread evenly over the base of the dish.
3. Just until the crust begins to turn a light shade of brown, bake for another 15 to 20 minutes.
4. Mix the eggs, sugar, gluten-free flour, baking soda, salt, lemon zest, and juice in a separate bowl.
5. Fry the crust first, then add the lemon mixture for the best results.
6. Check that the edges are crisp by baking for a further twenty-five minutes.
7. Wait at least two hours for the bars to cool in the pan before placing them in the fridge.
8. Powdered sugar can be sprinkled on top after cutting into squares.

Duration: forty five minutes

Nutrients: (Per Portion) Caloric content: 180, Amino content: 2g, Fat: 8g, Carb content: 26g, Fiber content: 1g

64. Gluten-Free Almond Flour Brownies

Ingredients:

- one cupful almond flour
- half cupful cocoa powder
- half teaspoonful baking soda
- one-fourth teaspoonful salt
- half cupful unsalted butter, melted
- one cupful granulated sugar
- two large eggs
- one teaspoonful vanilla extract
- half cupful gluten-free chocolate chips

Instructions:

1. It is necessary to bring the burner up to 175 degrees Celsius before using it (around 350 degrees Fahrenheit). Before you begin, grease and line a square baking dish.
2. Mix the almond flour, baking soda, cocoa powder, and salt together in a bowl.
3. In a another bowl, mix the powdered sugar and melted butter until thoroughly blended.
4. Add the eggs one by one and beat until well blended. Blend in the vanilla flavoring.
5. Toss the dry ingredients into the wet ones one by one and mix until everything is mixed.
6. Feel free to top it up with some gluten-free chocolate chips if you so like.
7. Once the pan is hot, pour in the batter.
8. When a toothpick inserted in the middle comes out with moist crumbs, bake for 25 to 30 minutes.
9. Before slicing into squares, let brownies cool completely in pan.

Duration: thirty minutes

Nutrients: (Per Portion) Caloric content: 200, Amino content: 3g, Fat: 12g, Carb content: 22g, Fiber content: 2g

65. Gluten-Free Raspberry Cheesecake Bars

Ingredients:

- one cupful gluten-free graham cracker crumbs
- one-fourth cupful unsalted butter, melted
- 1six oz cream cheese, softened
- half cupful granulated sugar
- two large eggs
- one teaspoonful vanilla extract
- half cupful raspberry jam

Instructions:

1. The stove must be preheated to 325 degrees Fahrenheit (160 C). Before you begin, grease and line a square baking dish.
2. You may make this recipe by combining melted butter with gluten-free graham cracker crumbs in a bowl. Spread evenly over the base of the dish.
3. Combine the granulated sugar and cream cheese in a big basin and stir until combined.
4. Add the eggs one by one and beat until well blended. Blend in the vanilla flavoring.

5. Once the graham crackers are arranged in a single layer, spread the cream cheese mixture on top.
6. The cream cheese layer can be topped with a tablespoon of raspberry jam.
7. Mix the jam and cream cheese by cutting into them with a knife.
8. To achieve a somewhat mushy middle and firm edges, bake for 35 to 40 minutes.
9. Wait at least two hours for the bars to cool in the pan before placing them in the fridge.
10. Before serving, cut into squares.

Duration: Forty minutes

Nutrients: (Per Portion) Caloric content: 220, Amino content: 4g, Fat: 15g, Carb content: 18g, Fiber content: 1g

66. Gluten-Free Apple Crisp

Ingredients:

- four cupful peeled and sliced apples
- two tablespoonful lemon juice
- half cupful granulated sugar
- one teaspoonful ground cinnamon
- one-fourth teaspoonful ground nutmeg
- one cupful gluten-free old-fashioned rolled oats
- half cupful almond flour
- one-fourth cupful chopped pecans
- one-fourth cupful unsalted butter, melted
- Vanilla ice cream for portion

Instructions:

1. It is necessary to bring the burner up to 175 degrees Celsius before using it (around 350 degrees Fahrenheit). Place a baking dish in the grease.
2. Peel and chop the apples, then place them in a big basin. Blend the spices, sugar, and lemon juice together (nutmeg and cinnamon).
3. Distribute the apple mixture evenly into the baking dish.
4. In a another bowl, mix together the melted butter, chopped almonds, almond flour, and gluten-free rolled oats. Combine the crumbs and mix thoroughly.
5. Arrange the apples on top of the oat mixture.
6. The apples should be soft and bubbling, with a golden brown topping, after 40 to 45 minutes in the oven.

7. Please let the apple crisp cool slightly before serving.
8. It is not necessary to have vanilla gelato.

Duration: forty five minutes

Nutrients: (Per Portion) Caloric content: 240, Amino content: 3g, Fat: 12g, Carb content: 34g, Fiber content: 5g

67. Gluten-Free Peanut Butter Blossoms

Ingredients:

- one cupful creamy peanut butter
- one cupful granulated sugar
- one large egg
- one teaspoonful vanilla extract
- half cupful gluten-free all-purpose flour
- half teaspoonful baking powder
- one-fourth teaspoonful salt
- 2four gluten-free chocolate Hershey's Kisses, unwrapped

Instructions:

1. It is necessary to bring the burner up to 175 degrees Celsius before using it (around 350 degrees Fahrenheit). Use parchment paper to line a baking pan.
2. In a bowl, mix together the peanut butter, whisk in the egg, granulated sugar, and vanilla essence.
3. Combine the salt, all-purpose gluten-free flour, baking powder, and flour in a separate bowl.
4. Combine the dry ingredients with the peanut butter mixture by gradually stirring in the dry ingredients.
5. After rolling the dough into balls about the size of an inch, set them on a baking sheet.
6. Once you've baked it for 10 to twelve minutes, the edges should be beautifully brown.
7. Immediately after removing the cookies from the oven, place a Hershey's Kiss in the center of each one.
8. The cookies should be removed from the baking pan and allowed to cool entirely on a wire rack after five minutes.

Duration: twelve minutes

Nutrients: (Per Portion) Caloric content: 120, Amino content: 3g, Fat: 7g, Carb content: 12g, Fiber content: 1g

68. Gluten-Free Banana Bread

Ingredients:

- two cupful mashed ripe bananas
- half cupful unsalted butter, melted
- half cupful granulated sugar
- two large eggs
- one teaspoonful vanilla extract
- two cupful gluten-free all-purpose flour
- one teaspoonful baking soda
- one-fourth teaspoonful salt
- half cupful chopped walnuts

Instructions:

1. It is necessary to bring the burner up to 175 degrees Celsius before using it (around 350 degrees Fahrenheit). Get a bread pan ready as you normally would by greasing and lining it.
2. Boil the butter, add the sugar, eggs, and vanilla extract to the mashed bananas in a big bowl.
3. Whisk together the salt, baking soda, and gluten-free all-purpose flour in separate bowls.
4. Whisk in the dry ingredients in a steady stream until combined with the banana mixture.
5. Add chopped walnuts if you like.
6. After preheating a loaf pan, pour in the batter.
7. Incorporate a toothpick into the center and bake for 55 to 60 minutes, or until it emerges clean.
8. Remove the banana bread from the pan and let it cool completely on a wire rack after ten minutes.

Duration: 60 minutes

Nutrients: (Per Portion) Caloric content: 200, Amino content: 3g, Fat: 10g, Carb content: 27g, Fiber content: 2g

69. Gluten-Free Blueberry Muffins

Ingredients:

- two cupful gluten-free all-purpose flour
- half cupful granulated sugar
- two teaspoonful baking powder
- half teaspoonful baking soda
- one-fourth teaspoonful salt
- one cupful buttermilk
- one-fourth cupful unsalted butter, melted
- two large eggs
- one teaspoonful vanilla extract
- one cupful fresh or frozen blueberries

Instructions:

1. Achieving a temperature of 190 degrees Celsius on the burner is the first step (about 375 degrees Fahrenheit). Line muffin tins with paper liners.
2. The gluten-free all-purpose flour can be made by whisking together sugar, baking soda, baking powder, and salt in a large bowl.
3. Combine the eggs, buttermilk, melted butter, and vanilla essence in a separate bowl and whisk to combine.
4. Slowly add the liquid components to the dry ones while stirring constantly until barely combined.
5. Stir in the blueberries gently.
6. About three quarters of the way into the muffin pan should be batter.
7. After another 18–20 minutes in the oven, insert a toothpick to test for doneness.

8. Remove the muffins from the pan and let them cool completely on a wire rack after five minutes.

Duration: twenty minutes

Nutrients: (Per Portion) Caloric content: 180, Amino content: 3g, Fat: 6g, Carb content: 28g, Fiber content: 1g

70. Gluten-Free Chocolate Avocado Mousse

Ingredients:

- two ripe avocados, peeled and pitted
- half cupful cocoa powder
- half cupful maple syrup
- one teaspoonful vanilla extract
- Pinch of salt
- Fresh berries for garnish

Instructions:

1. Choco powder, maple syrup, vanilla essence, ripe avocados, and a bit of salt should be blended or processed until smooth.
2. To make a smooth and creamy consistency, blend the ingredients together.
3. The chocolate avocado mousse needs at least an hour to chill in the fridge before it can be served.
4. Before serving, divide the mousse among individual bowls and top with berries.

Preparation Time: ten minutes

Chilling Time: one hour

Nutrients: (Per Portion) Caloric content: 180, Amino content: 3g, Fat: 10g, Carb content: 25g, Fiber content: 6g

Conclusion

As this gluten-free cookbook comes to an end, it's vital to reflect on the profound impact going gluten-free has had on your life. After reading the introduction chapters and giving the many recipes a go, you should now be well-versed in the nuances of gluten, have a healthy gluten-free kitchen under your belt, and know how to make tasty gluten-free meals.

A comprehensive examination of gluten's origins, properties, and implications for those with celiac disease or sensitivity was the first stop on the journey. Now that you know what gluten sensitivity symptoms are and how celiac disease works, you have a solid grasp of the many aspects of gluten-related health problems.

Finding one's way around a gluten-free pantry became an art form as one learned to identify essential gluten-free ingredients and effortlessly substitute gluten in standard recipes. Acquiring expert-level label reading skills will empower you to confidently peruse the aisles, evade possible gluten sources, and ensure that your recipes adhere to your diet.

Your gluten-free kitchen is ready for action, and you've taken great care to arrange your workspace and kitchen with all the tools you'll need. Everything is in place for a satisfying and healthy gluten-free culinary adventure thanks to your meticulously planned meals.

The prospect of a delectable adventure is enticed by each recipe chapter, beginning with Morning Bliss and ending with Sweet Endings. Not only do these recipes meet your dietary restrictions, they also take gluten-free food to a whole new level. From the exotic Gluten-Free Quinoa and Vegetable Stir-Fry to the comforting Gluten-Free Shepherd's Pie, every dish highlights the variety and creativity that comes with gluten-free cuisine.

No ordinary cookbook—this gluten-free tome is an ode to flavor, an ode to good health, and an ode to the joy of making food that nourishes more than just the stomach. May the recipes in this cookbook ignite your creativity as you embark on this culinary journey and ensure that every meal is a delight and fulfills your hunger.

With all the new information and tasty recipes you've accumulated, going gluten-free is more than just a choice; it's an adventure in culinary discovery. Cheers to a future when everyone can enjoy tasty, nutritious, and gluten-free sweets!

www.ingramcontent.com/pod-product-compliance
Lightning Source LLC
LaVergne TN
LVHW070205080526
838202LV00063B/6563